HOUSE OF BOO
COLORING BOOK

BY: JENN POLK

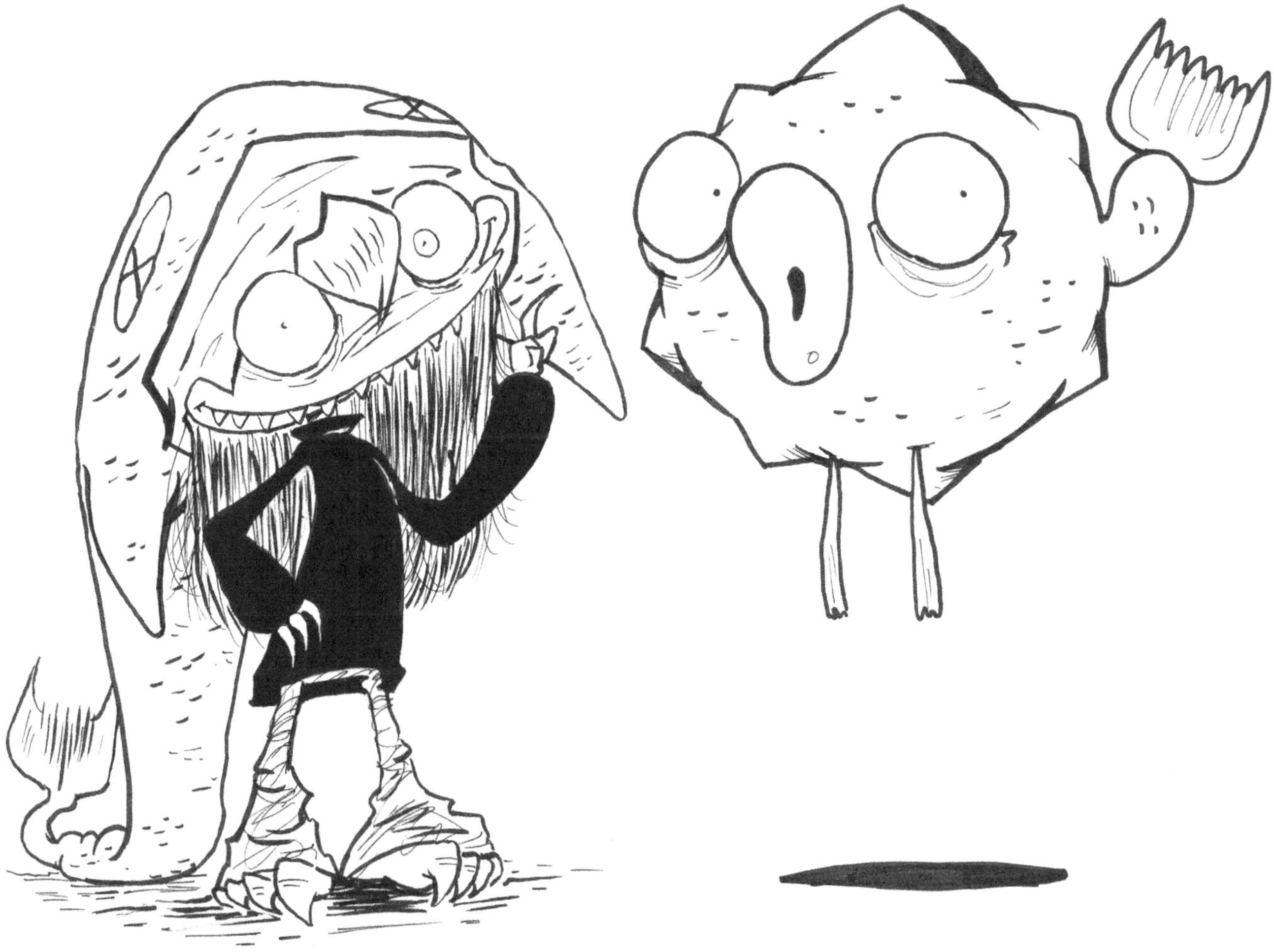

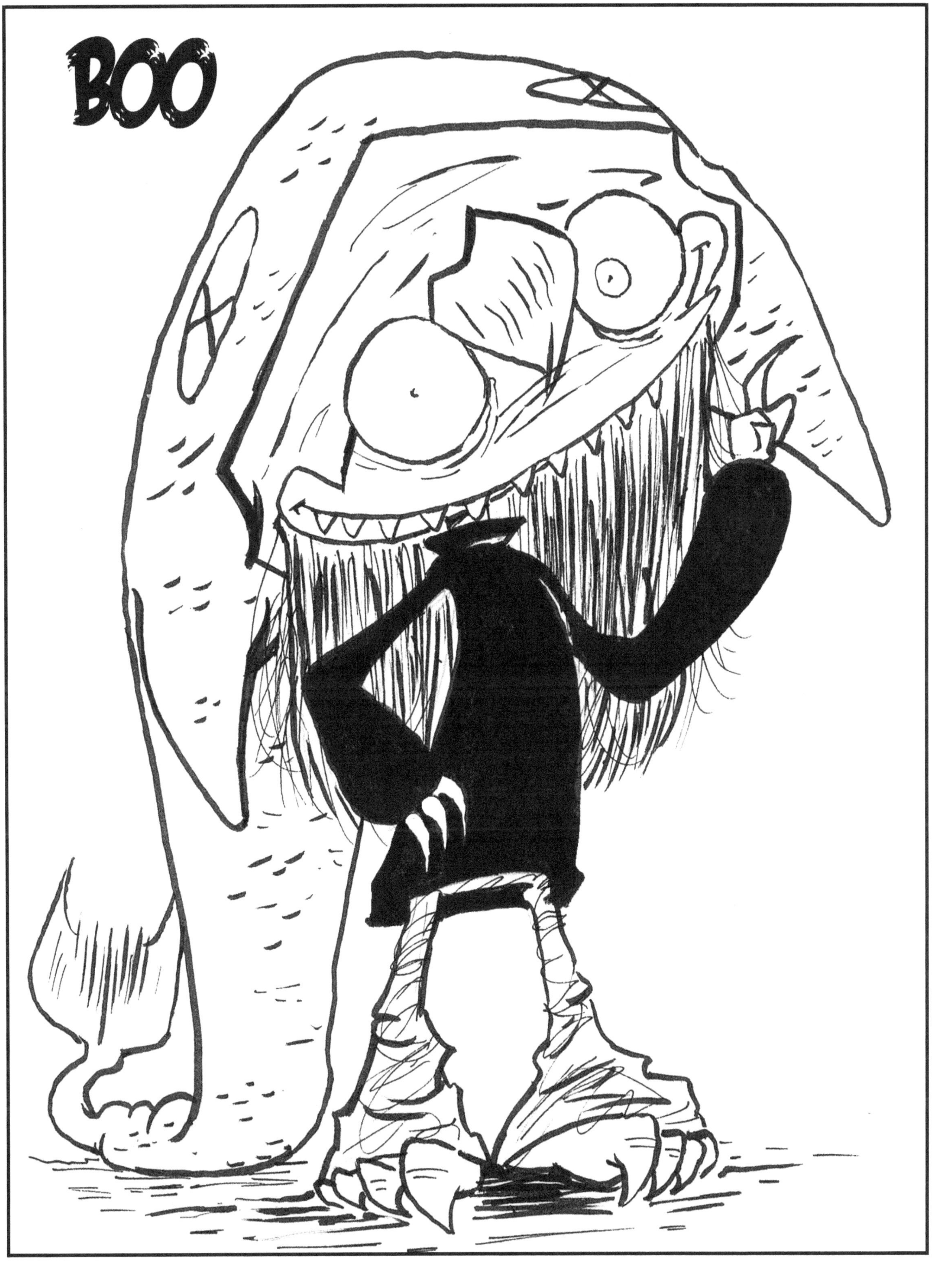
BOO

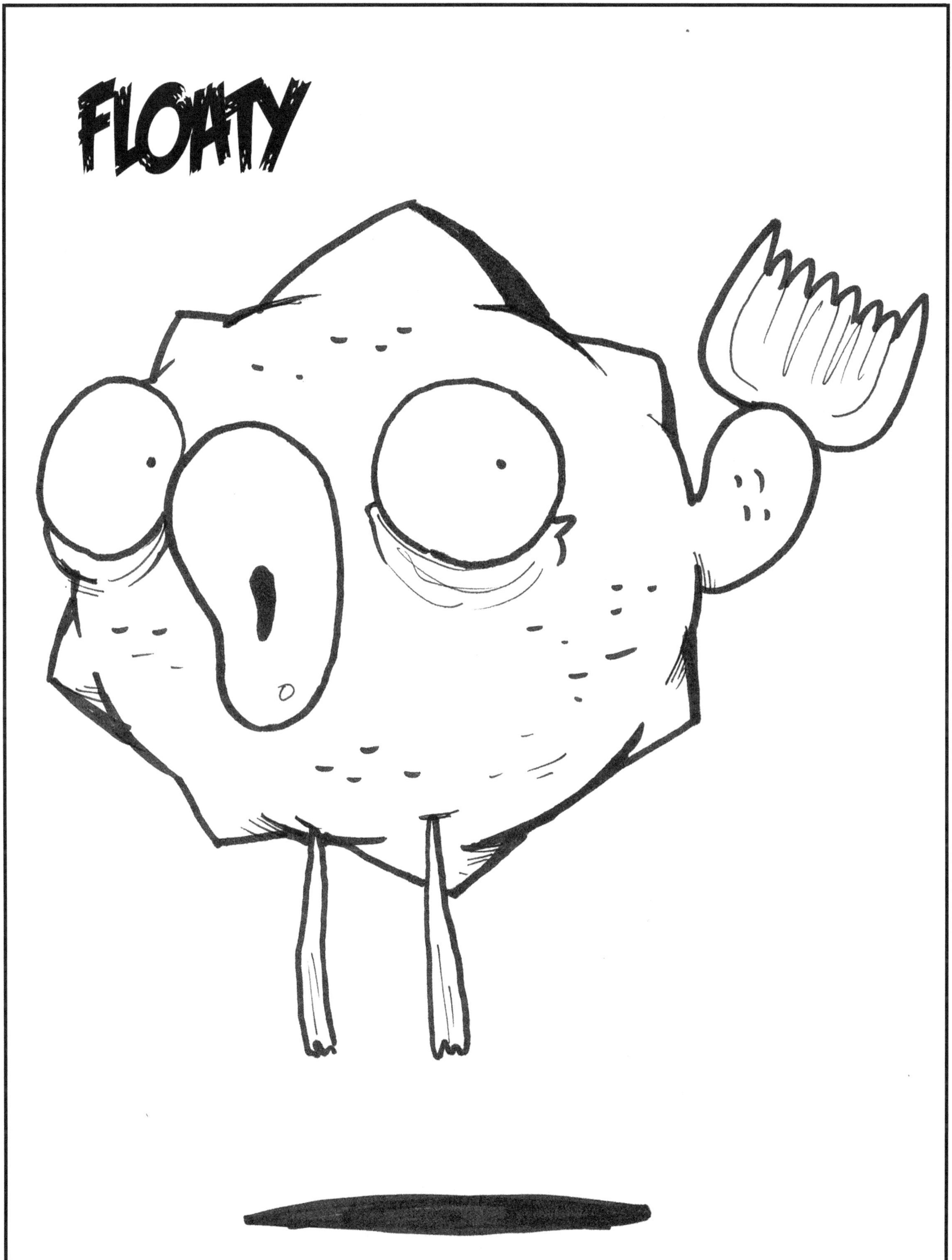
FLOATY

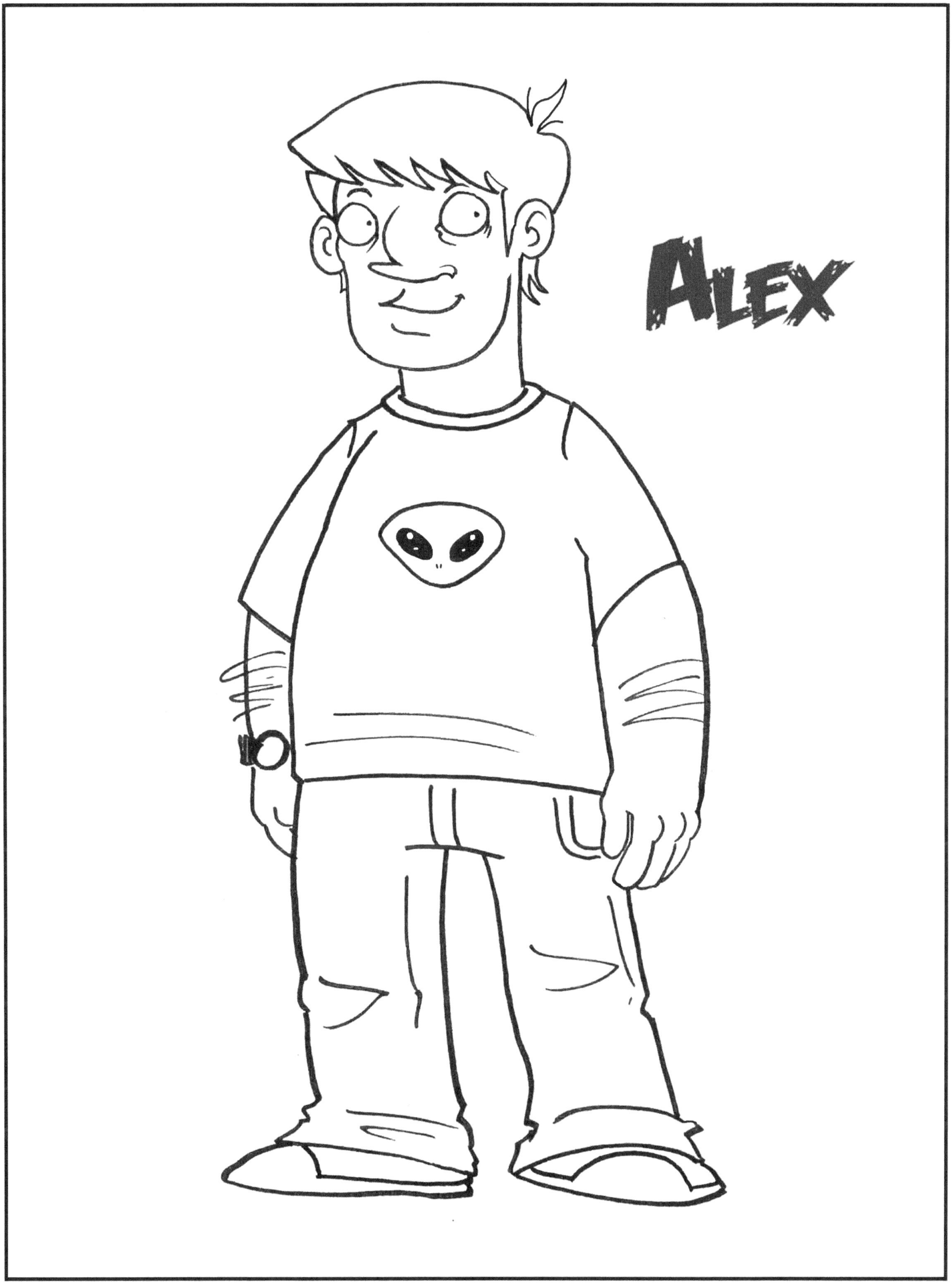
ALEX

MR BOGEYMAN

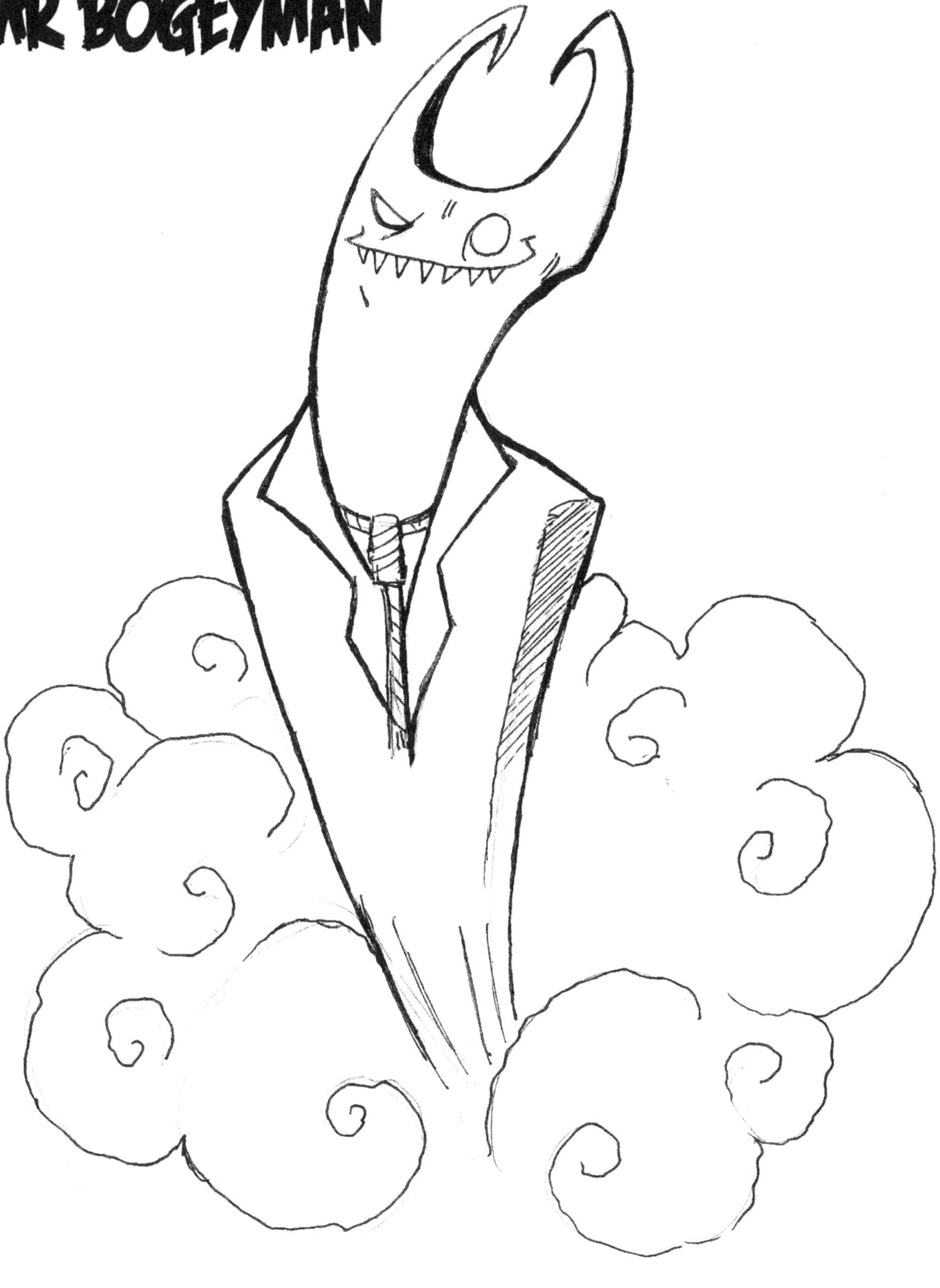

GRAMPUS

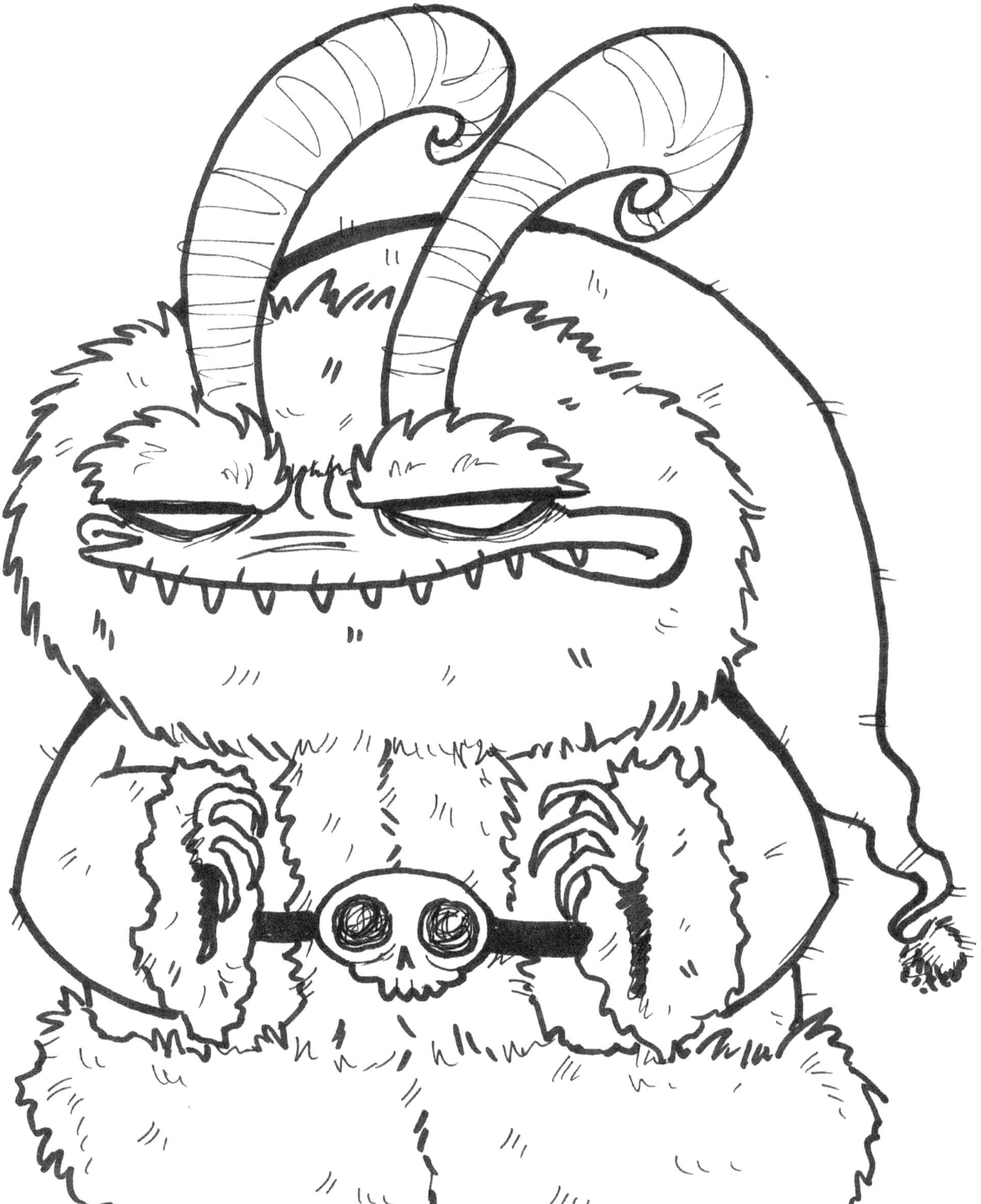

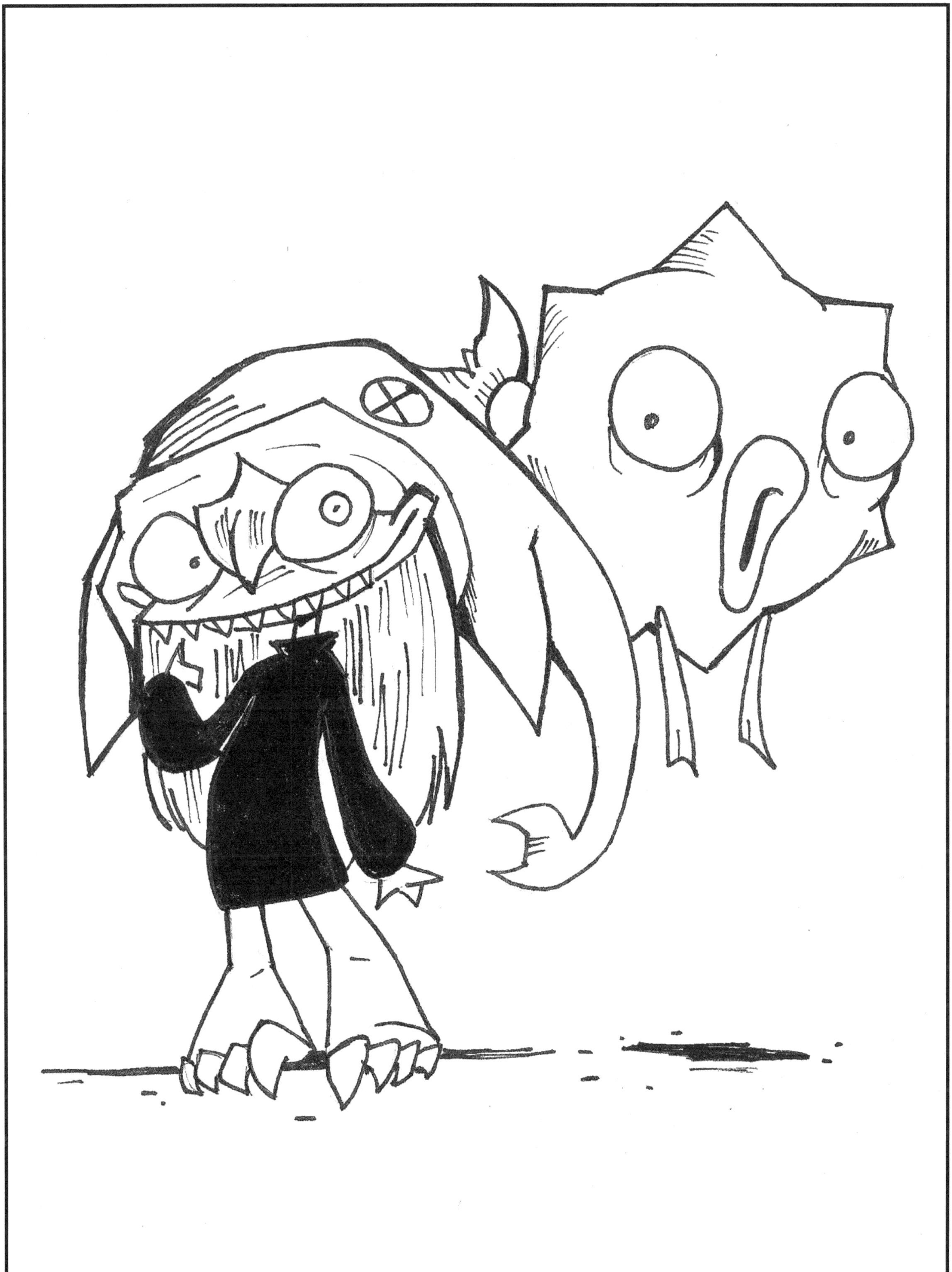

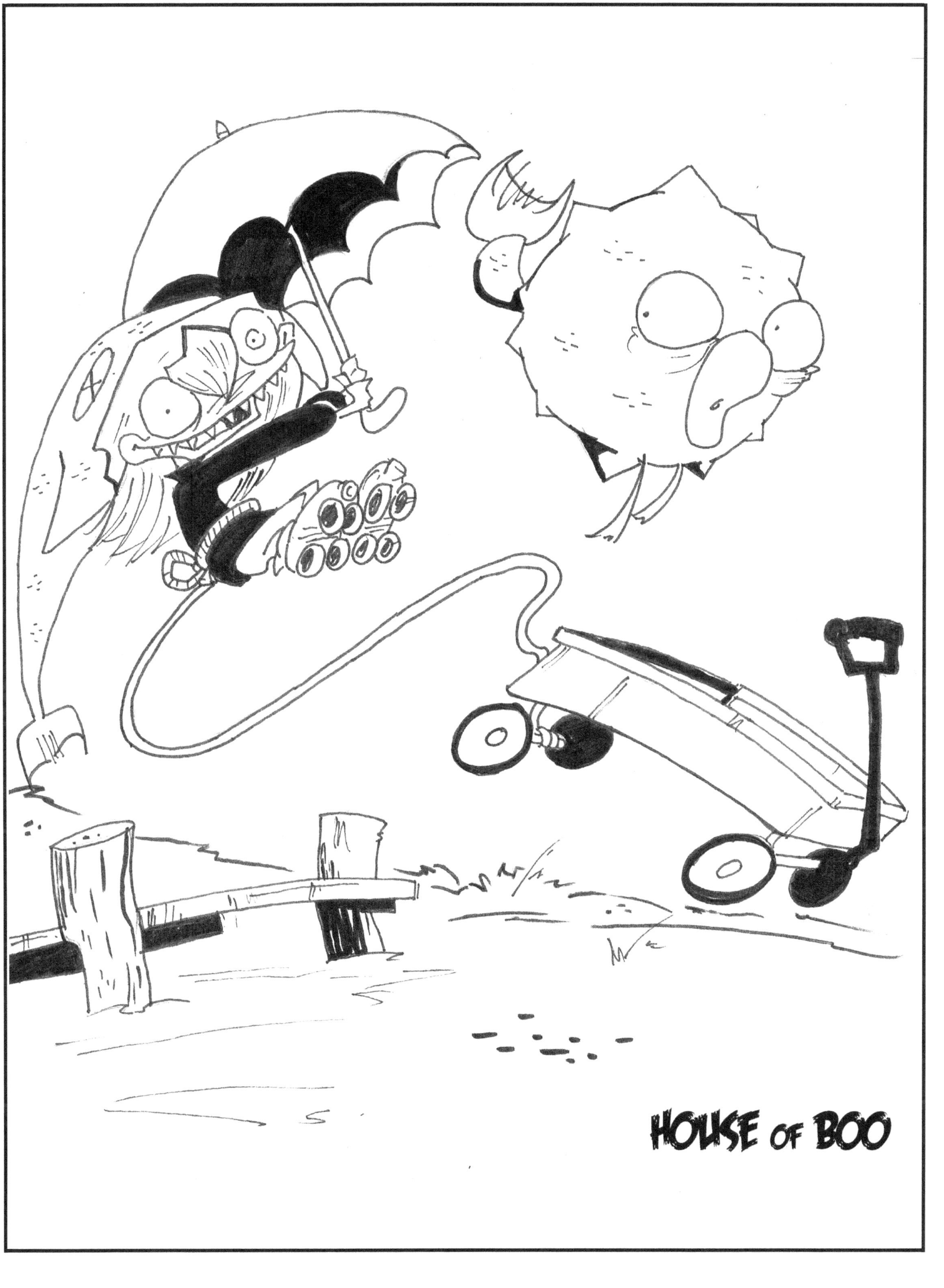
HOUSE OF BOO

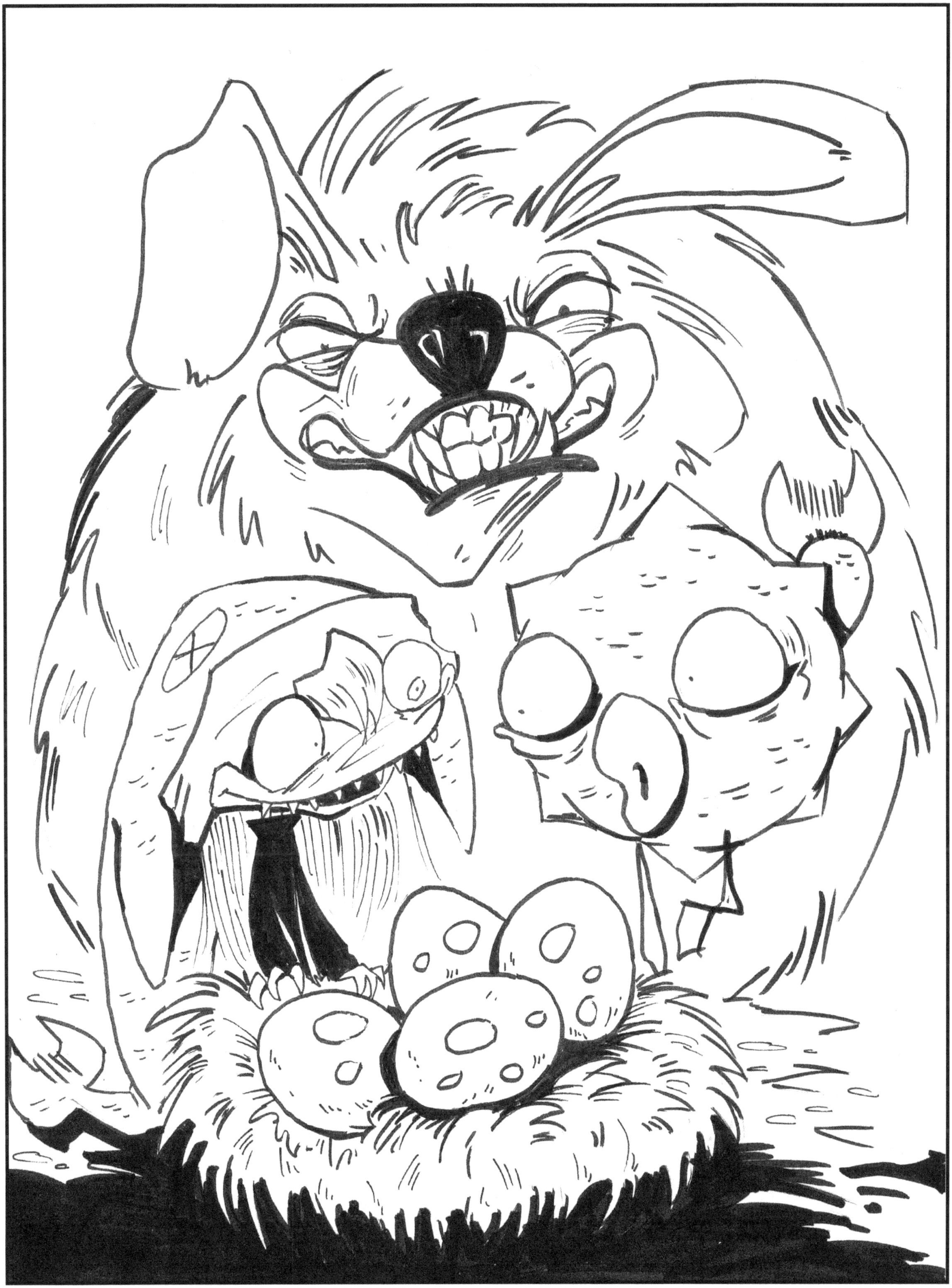

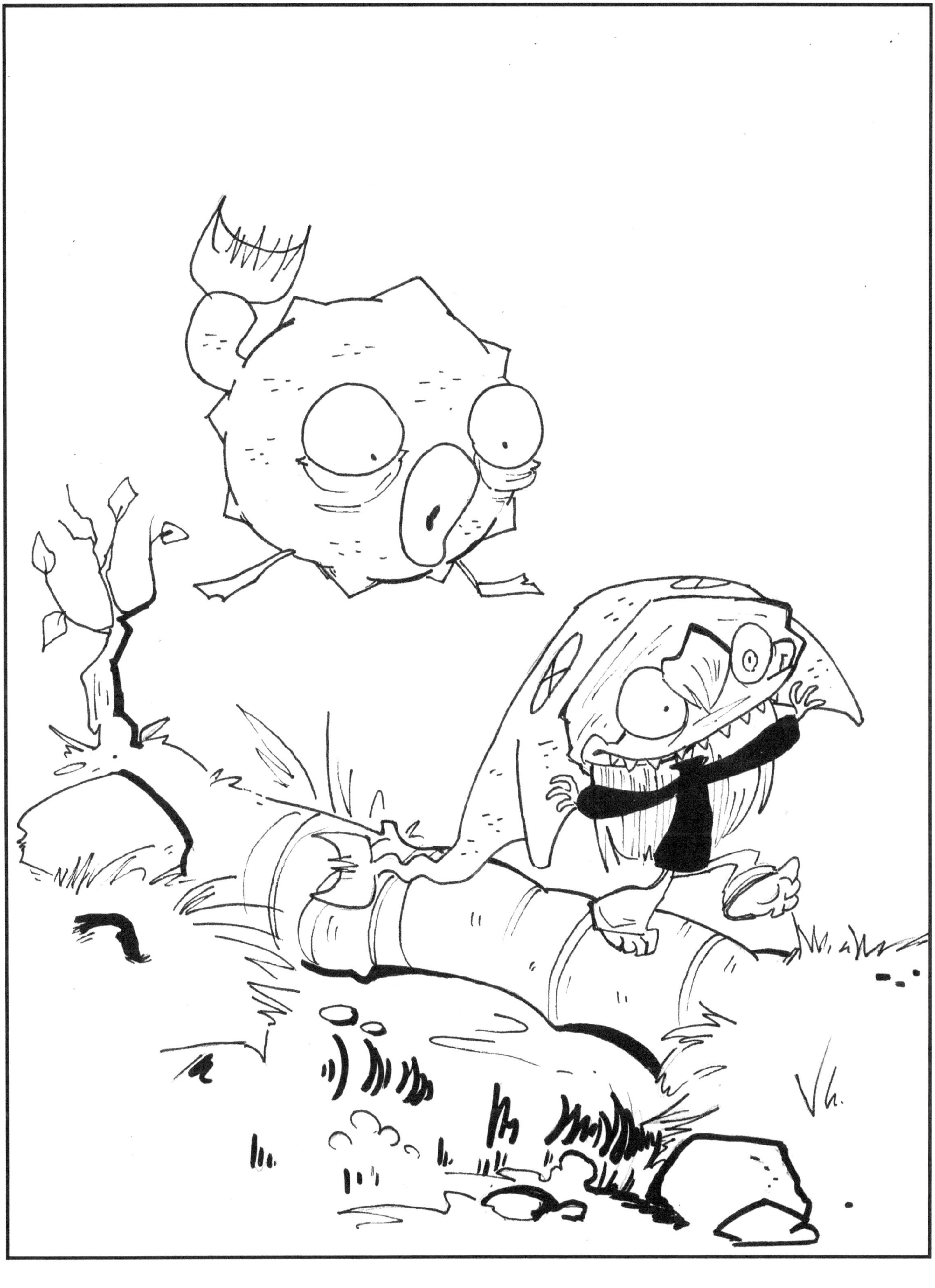

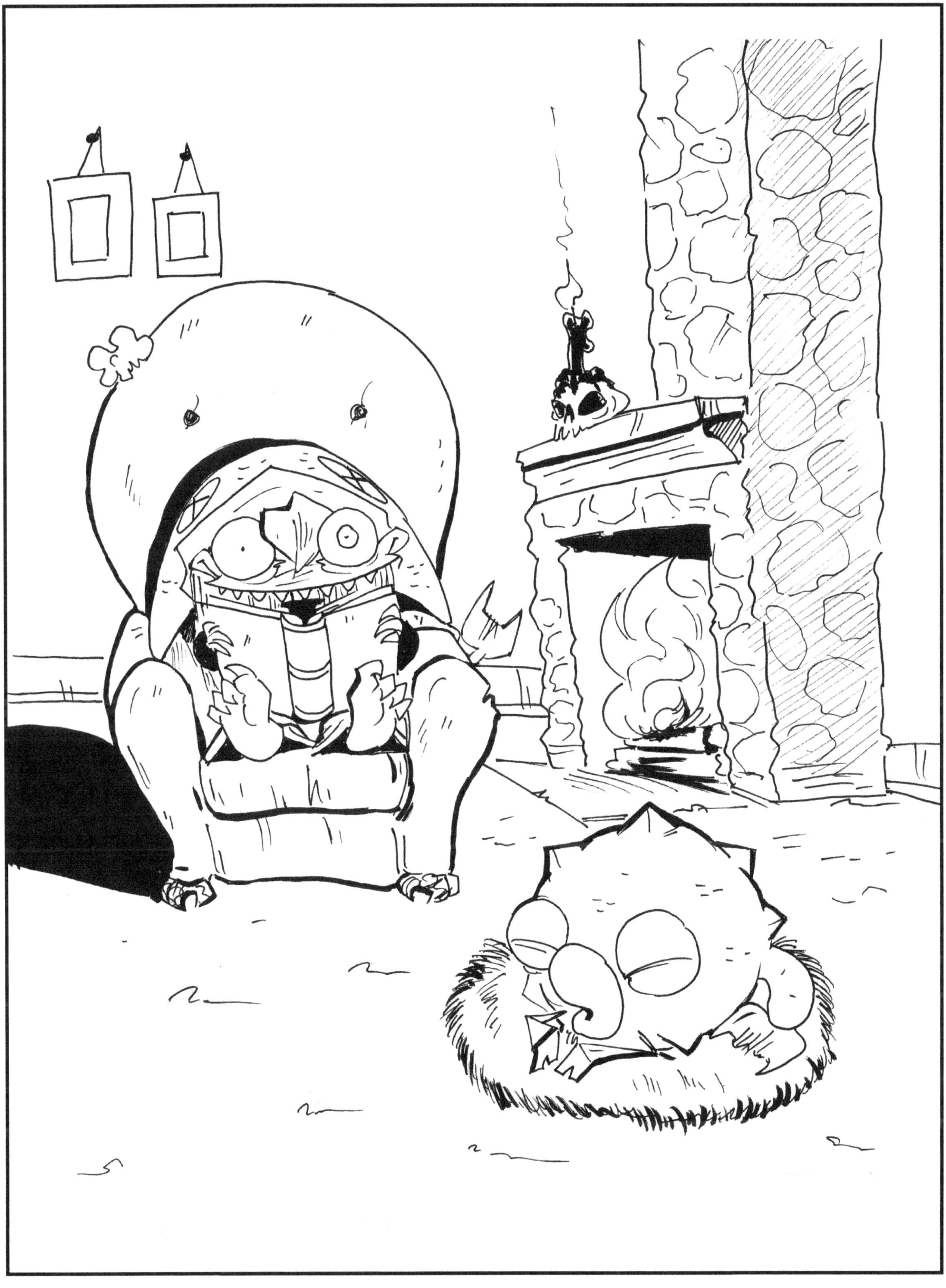

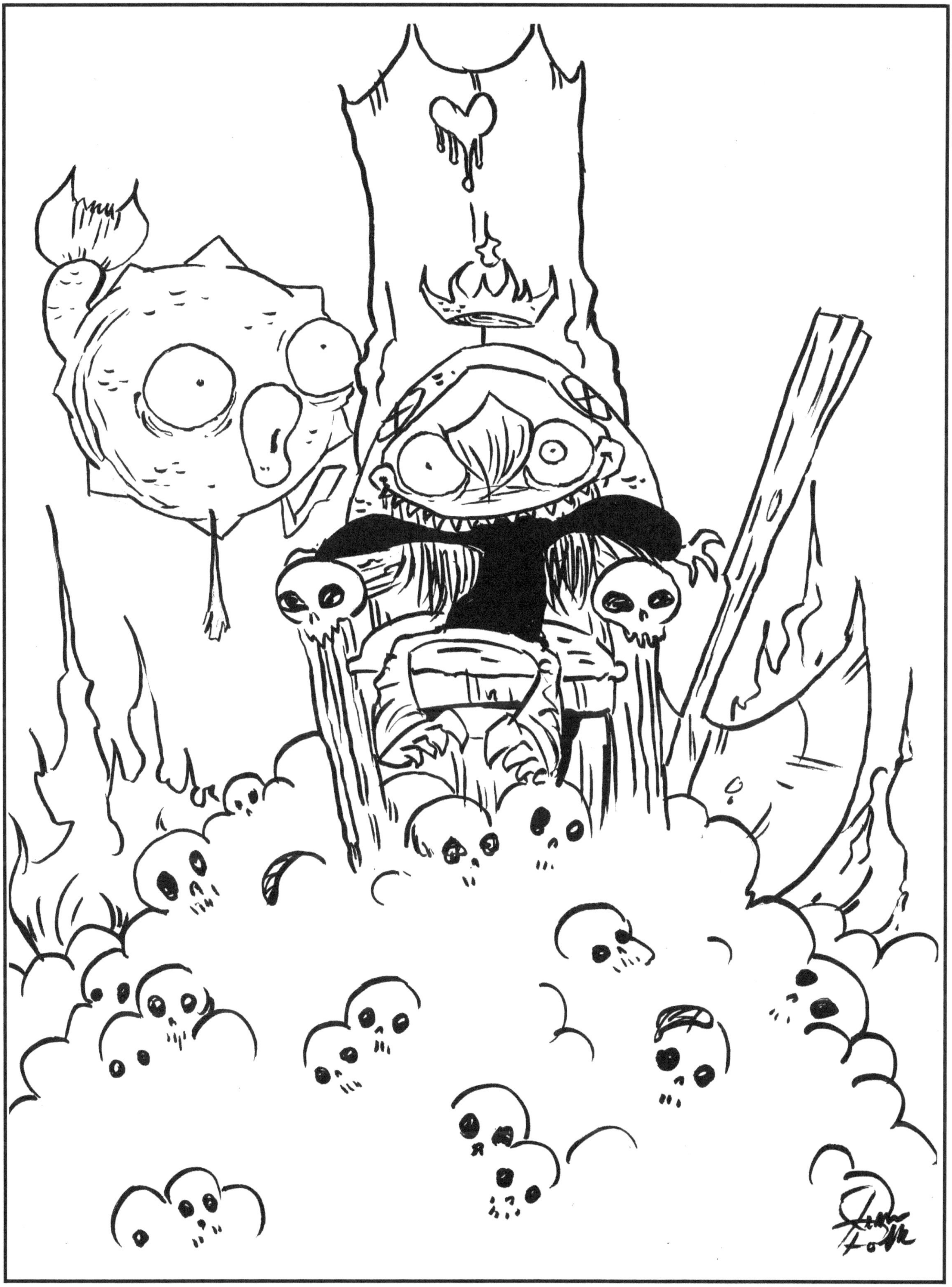

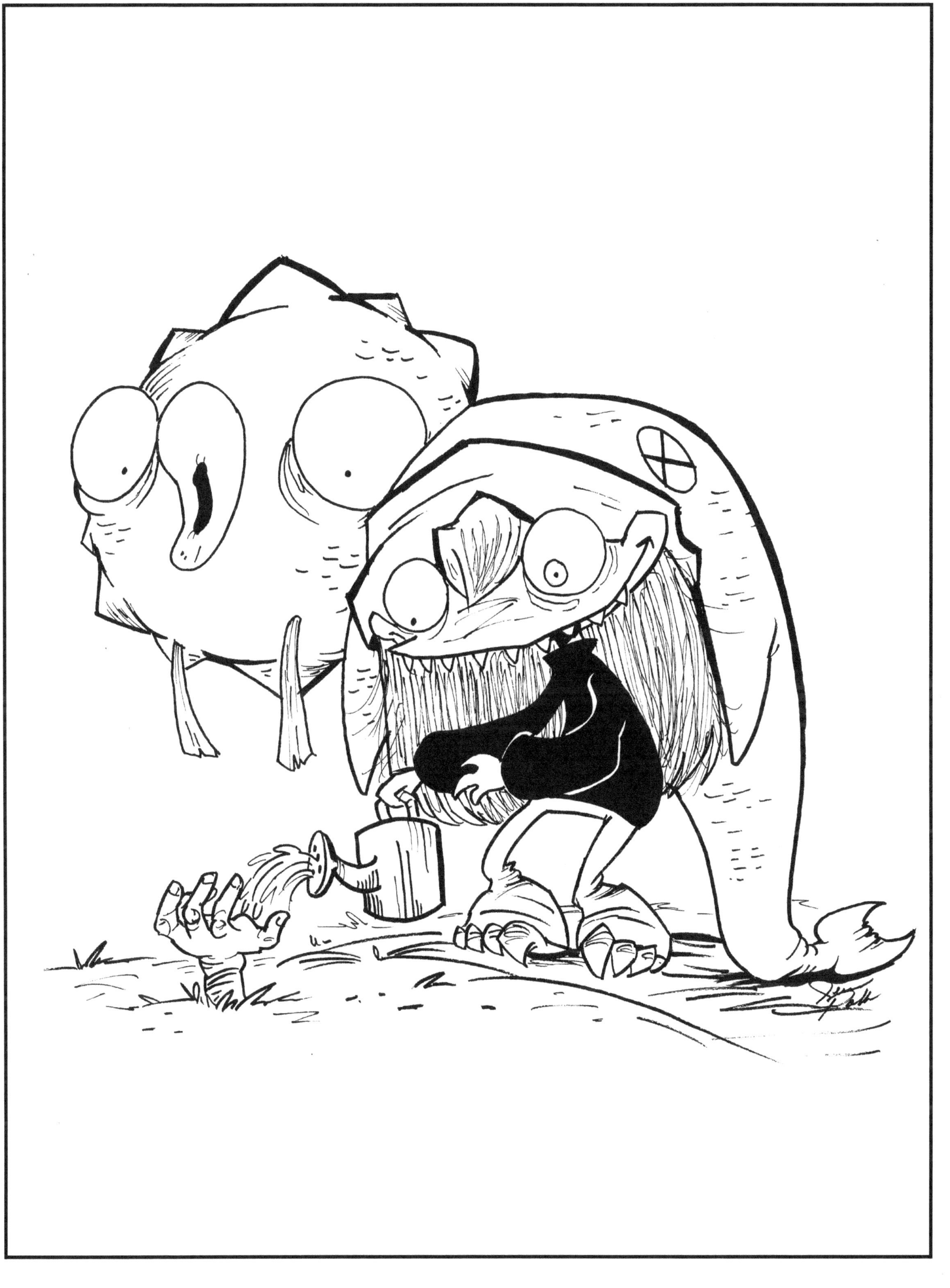

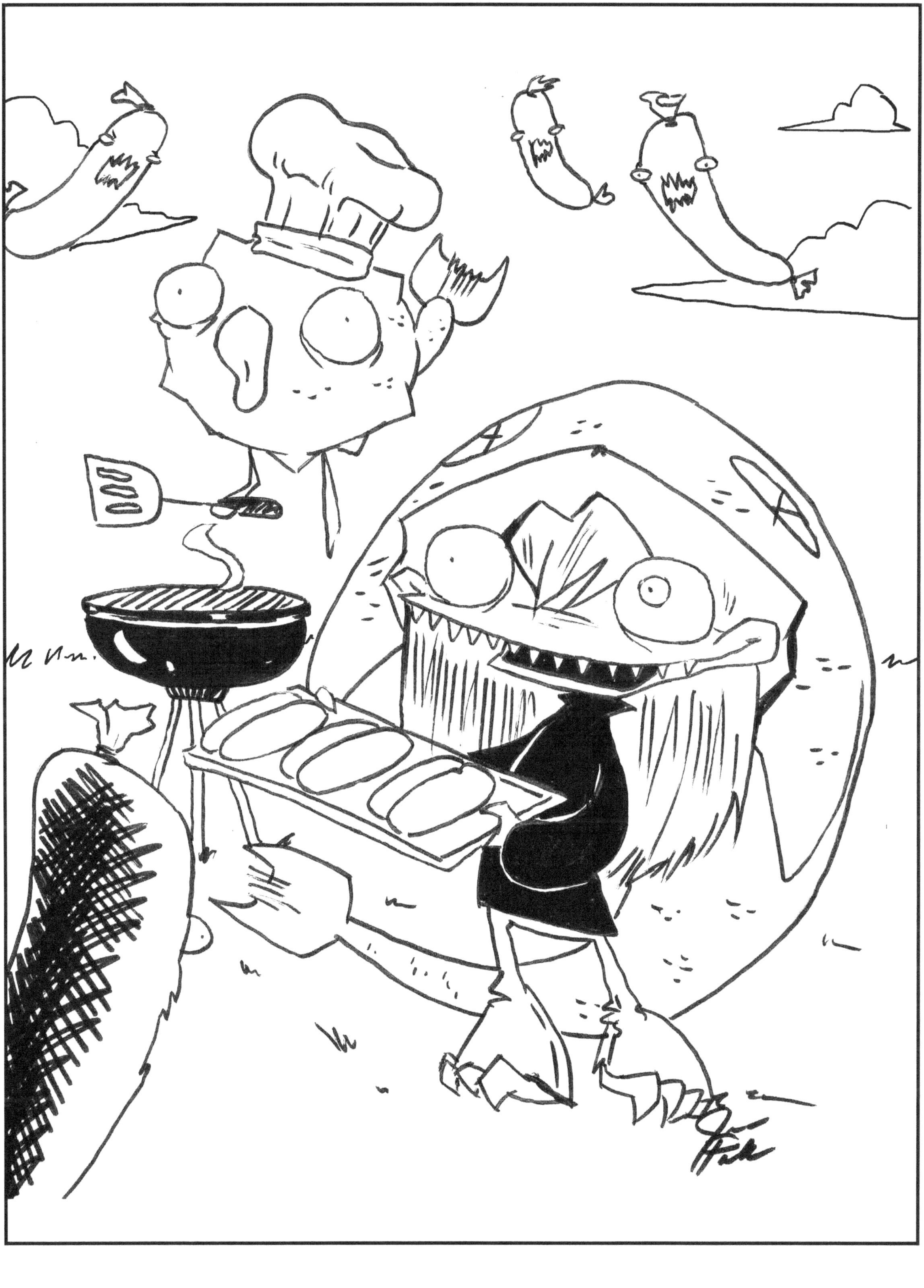

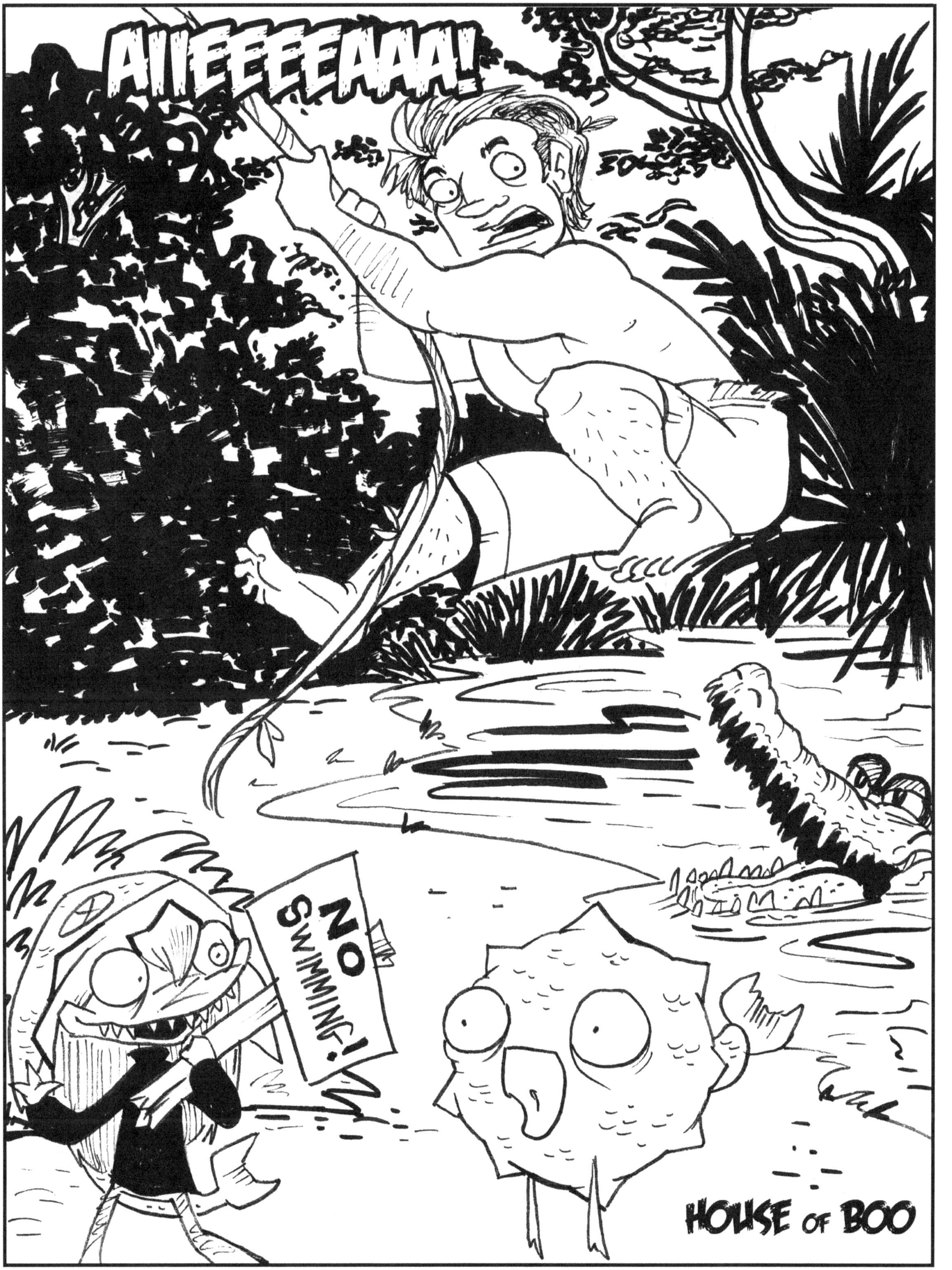
AIIEEEEEAAA!
NO SWIMMING!
HOUSE OF BOO

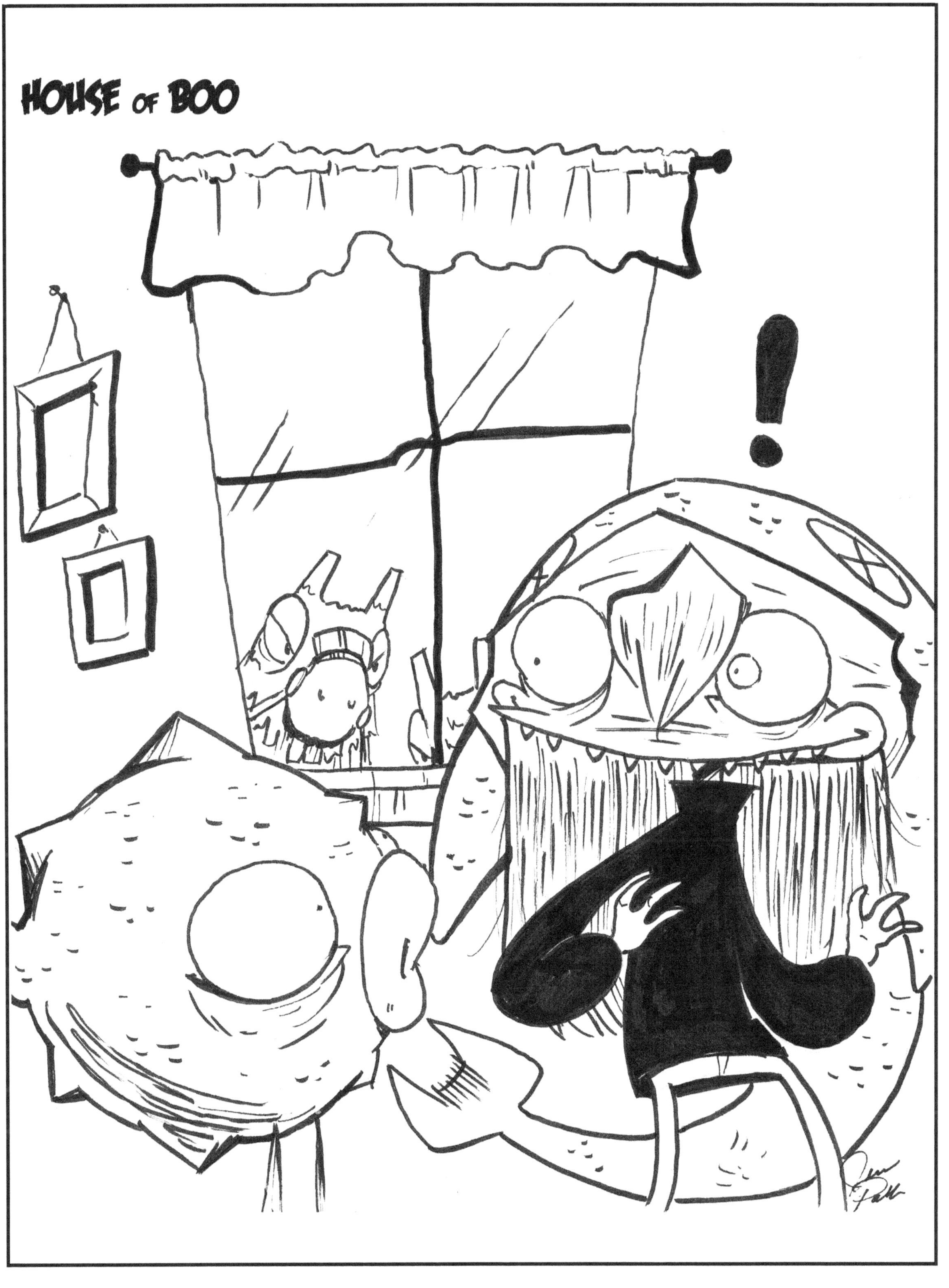
HOUSE OF BOO
!

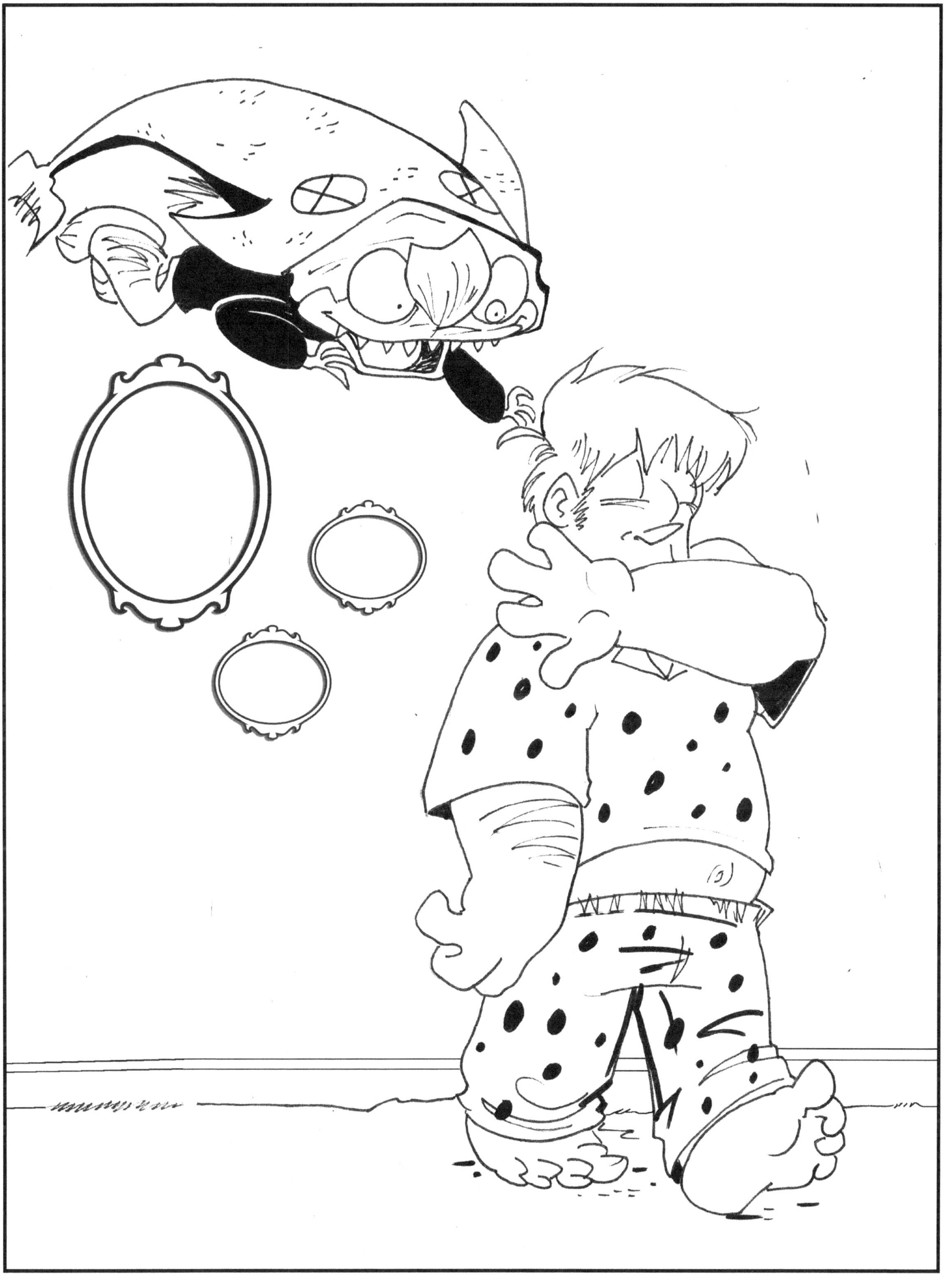

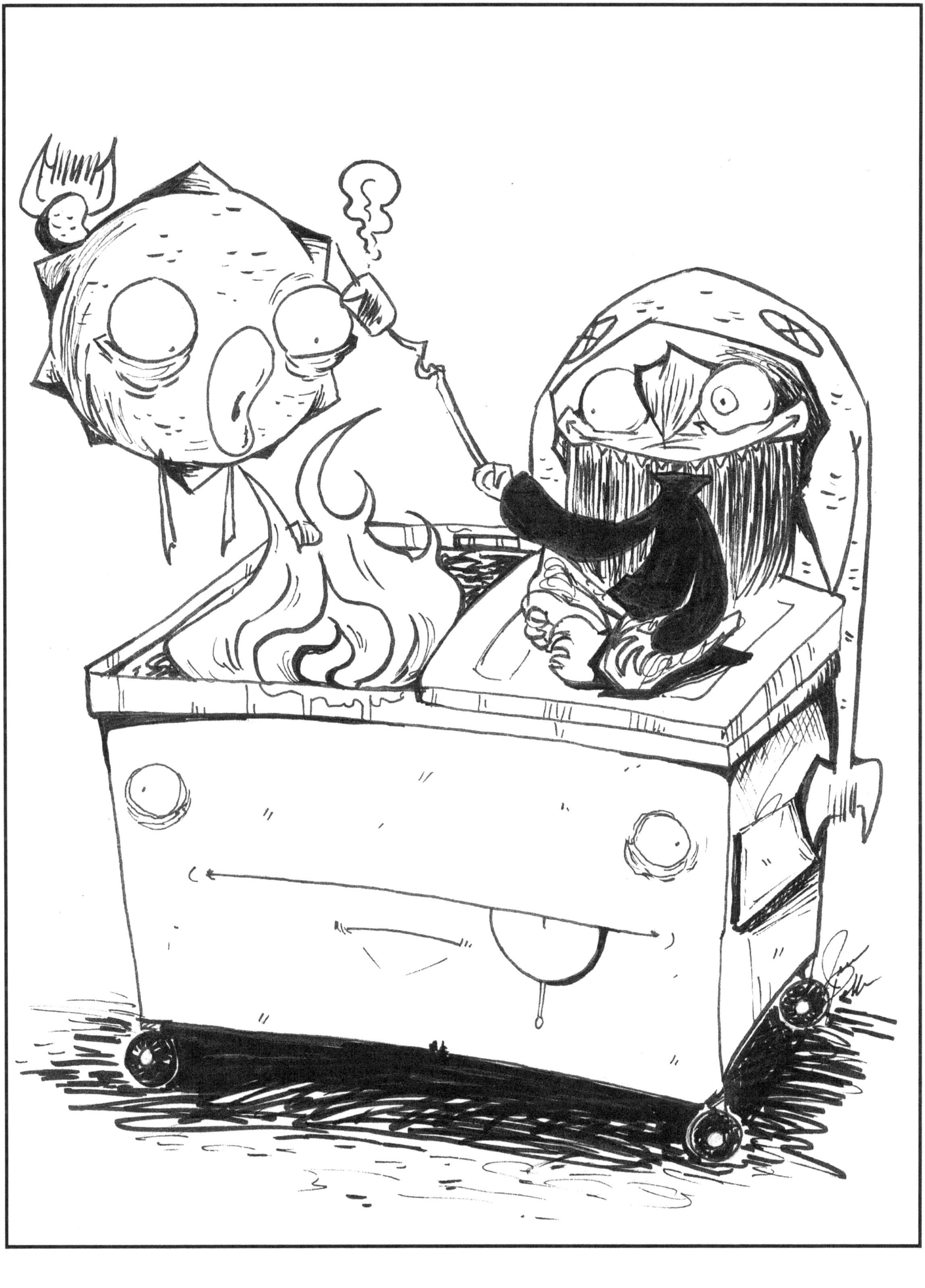

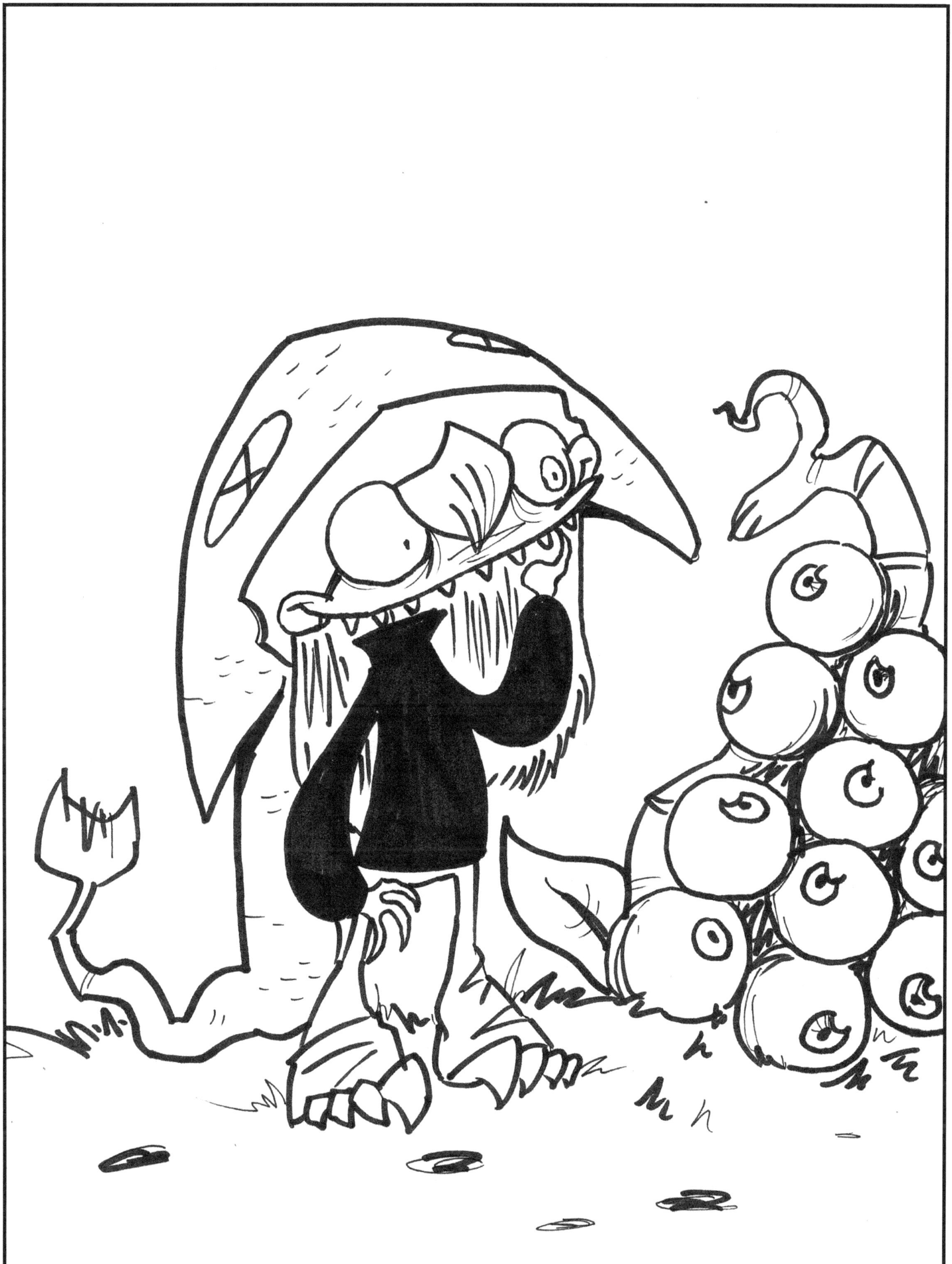

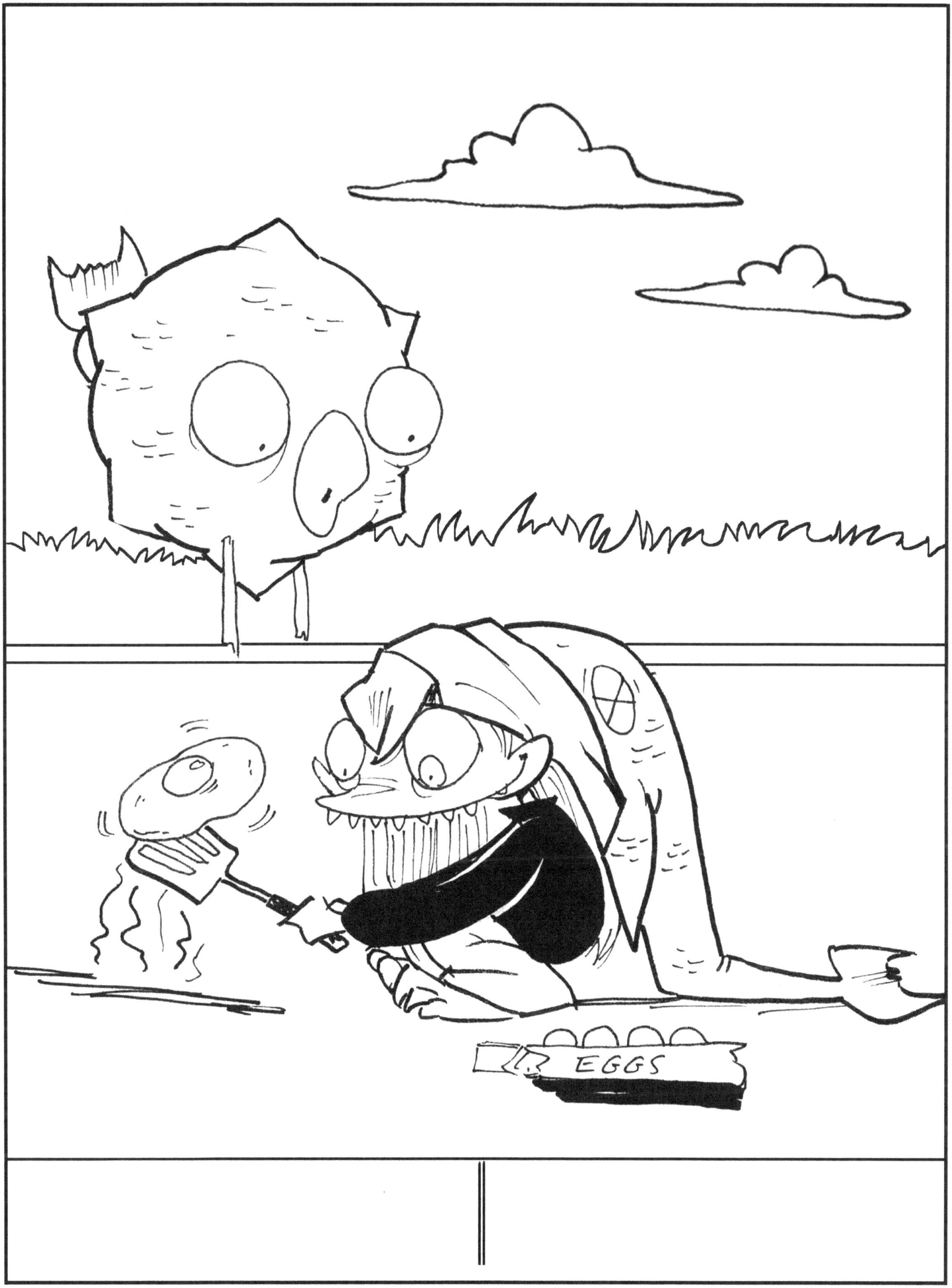
EGGS

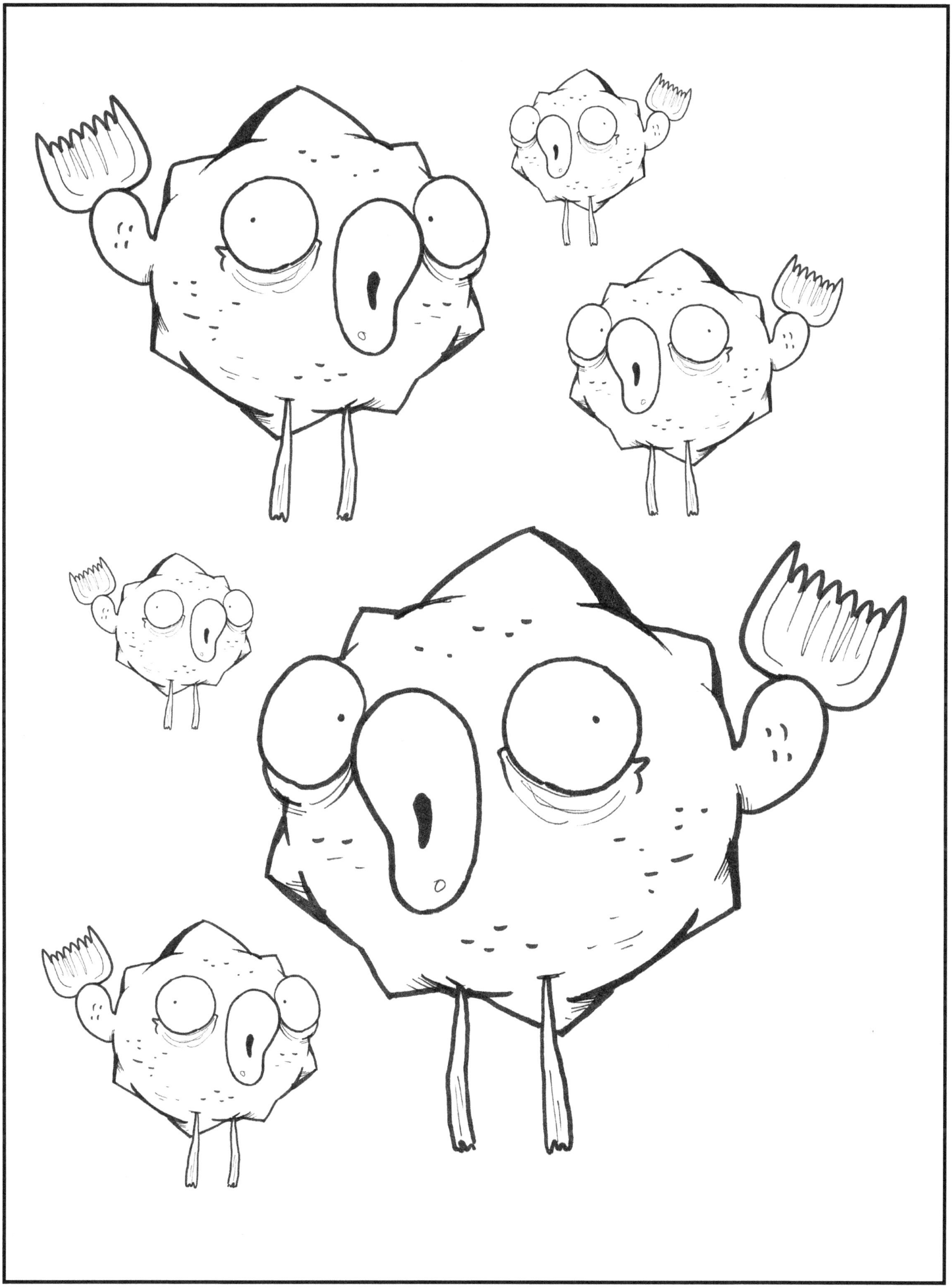

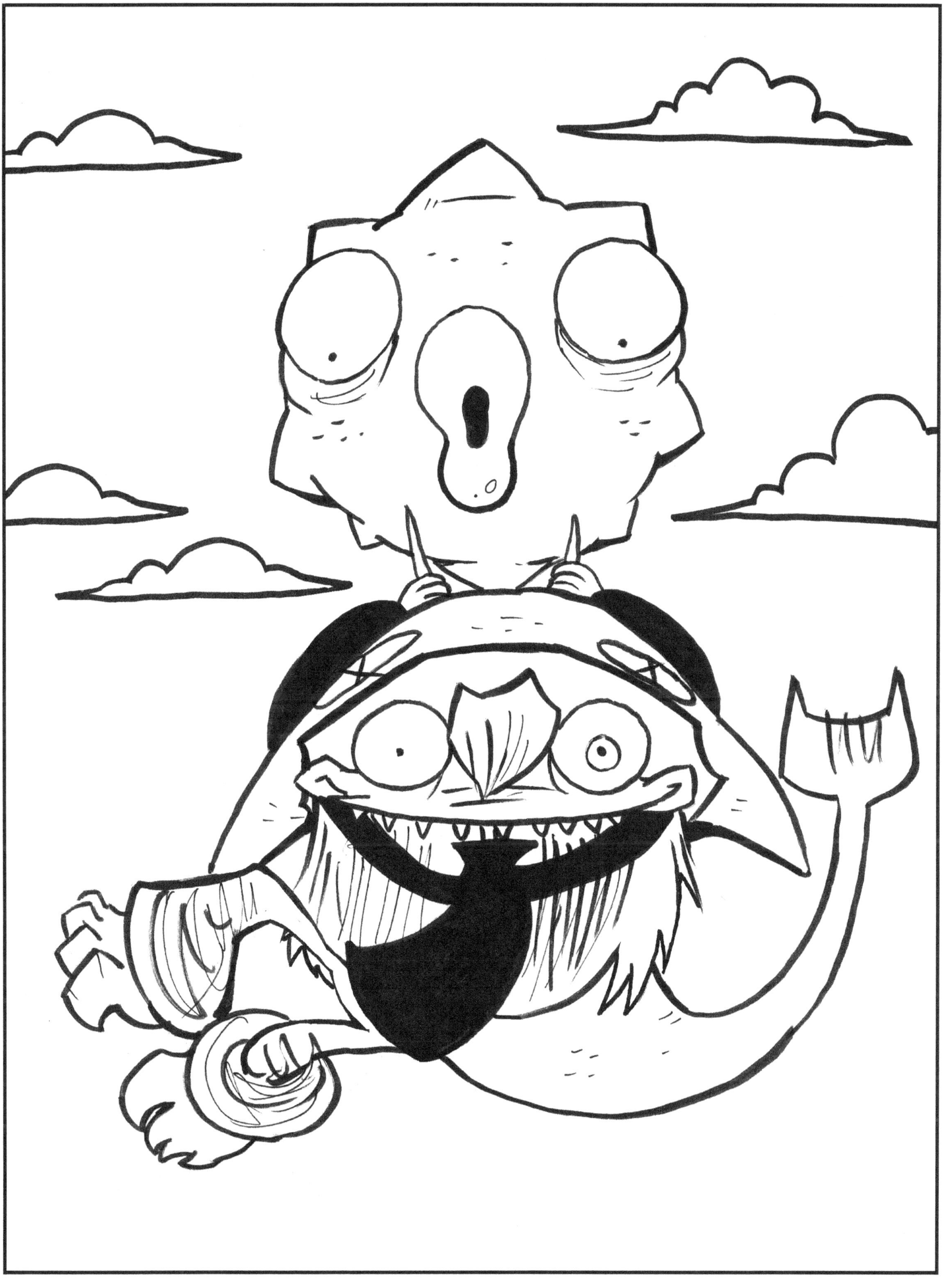

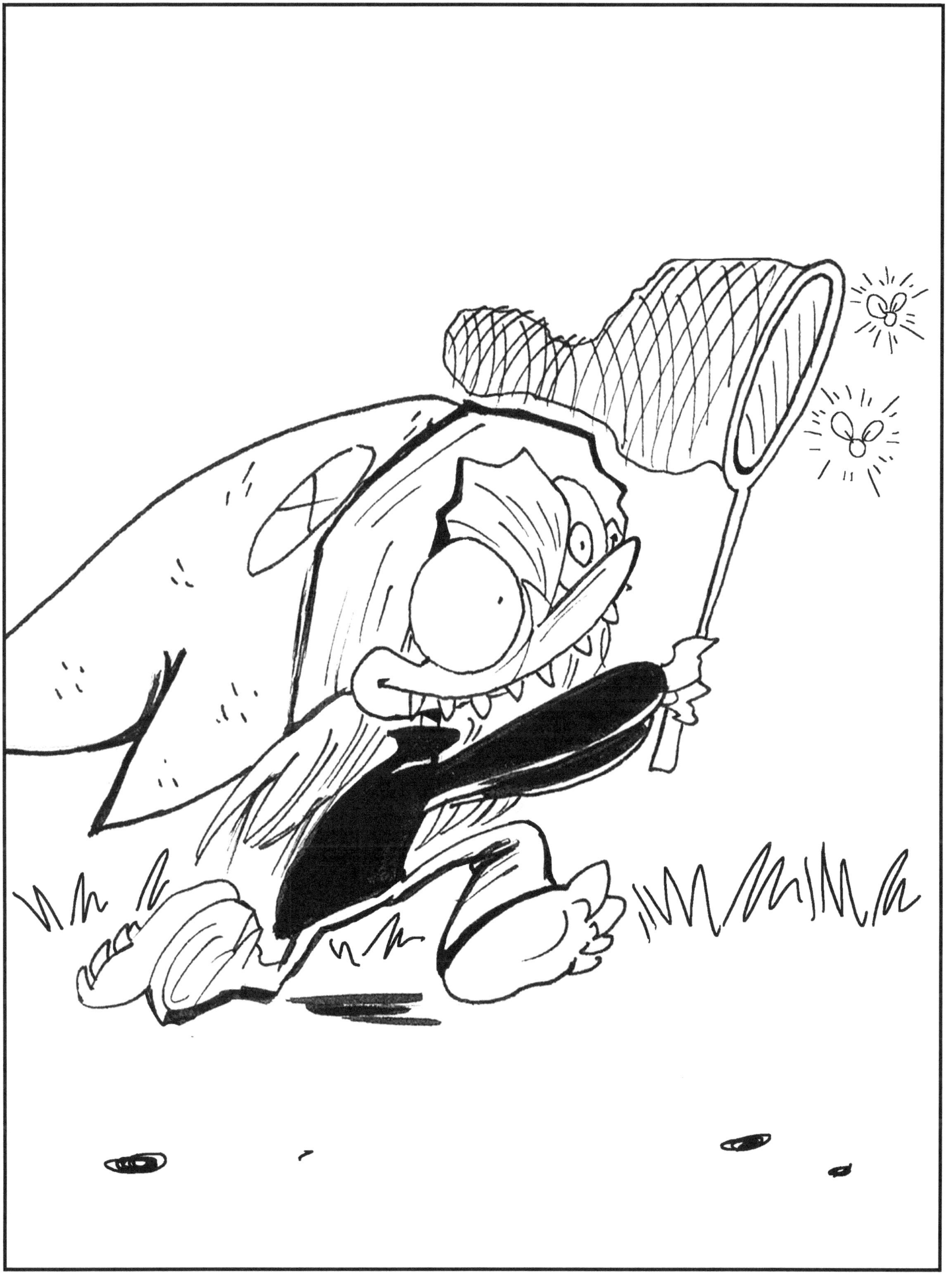

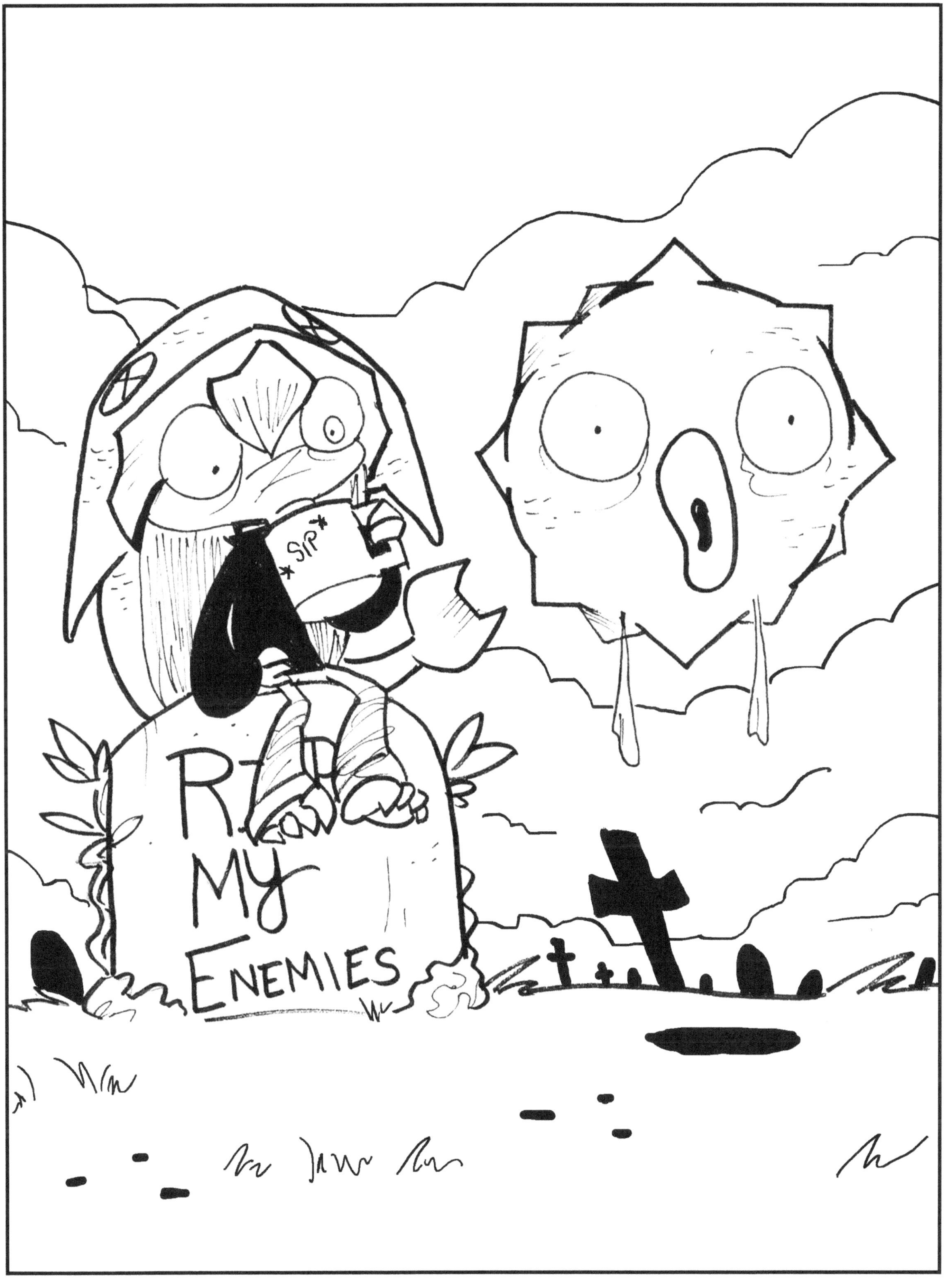
SIP
MY
ENEMIES

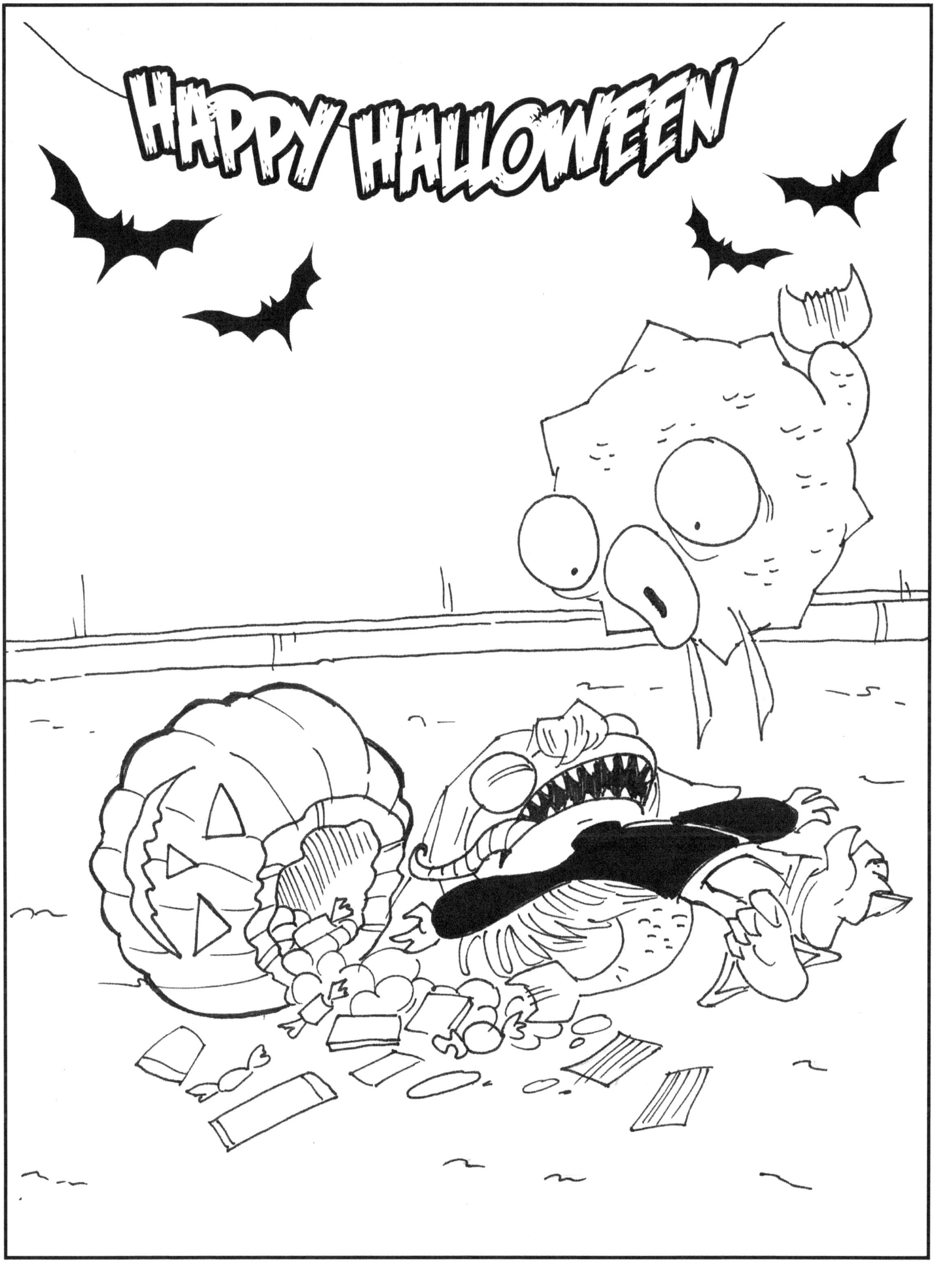
HAPPY HALLOWEEN

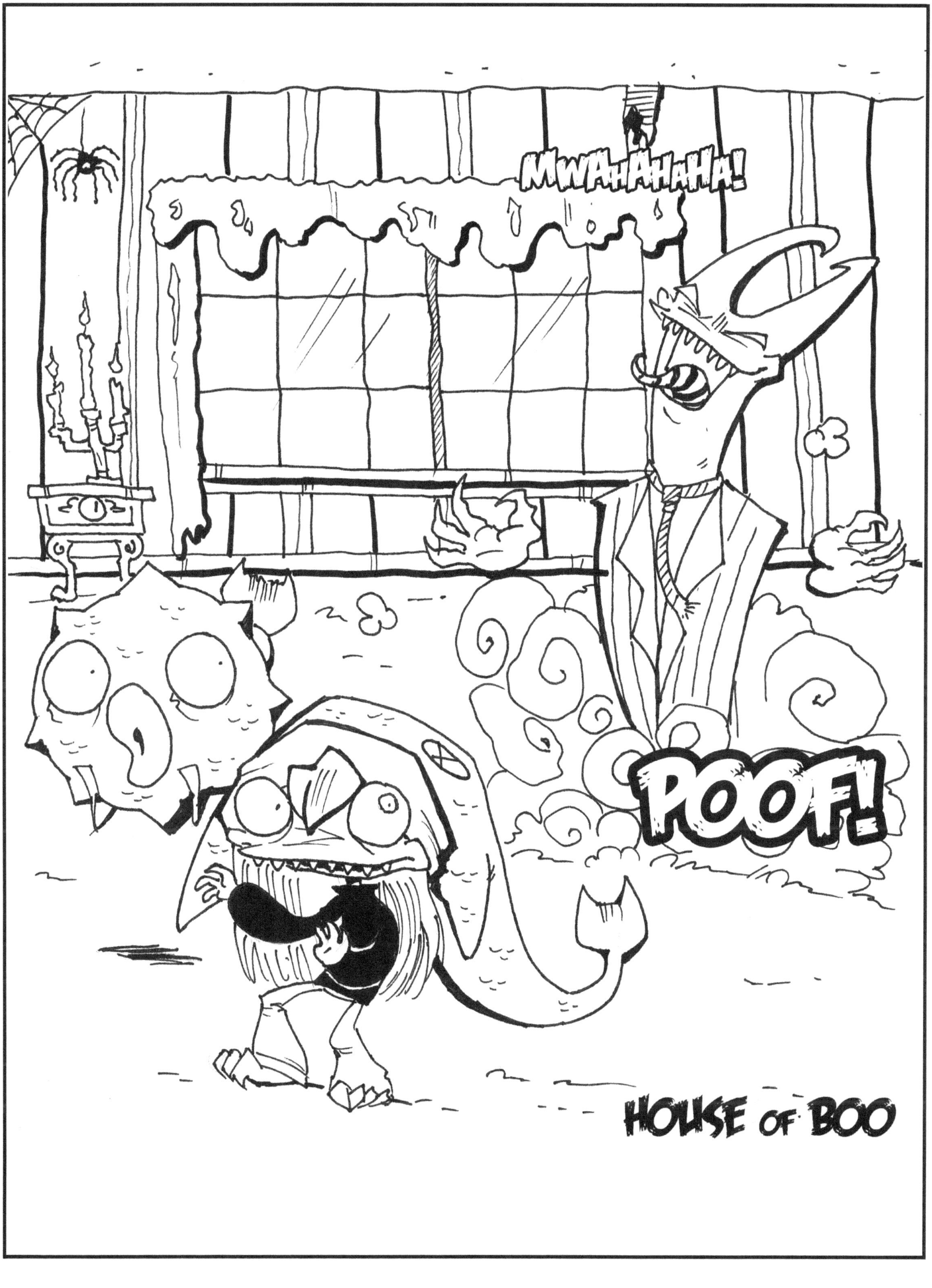
MWAHAHAHA!
POOF!
HOUSE OF BOO

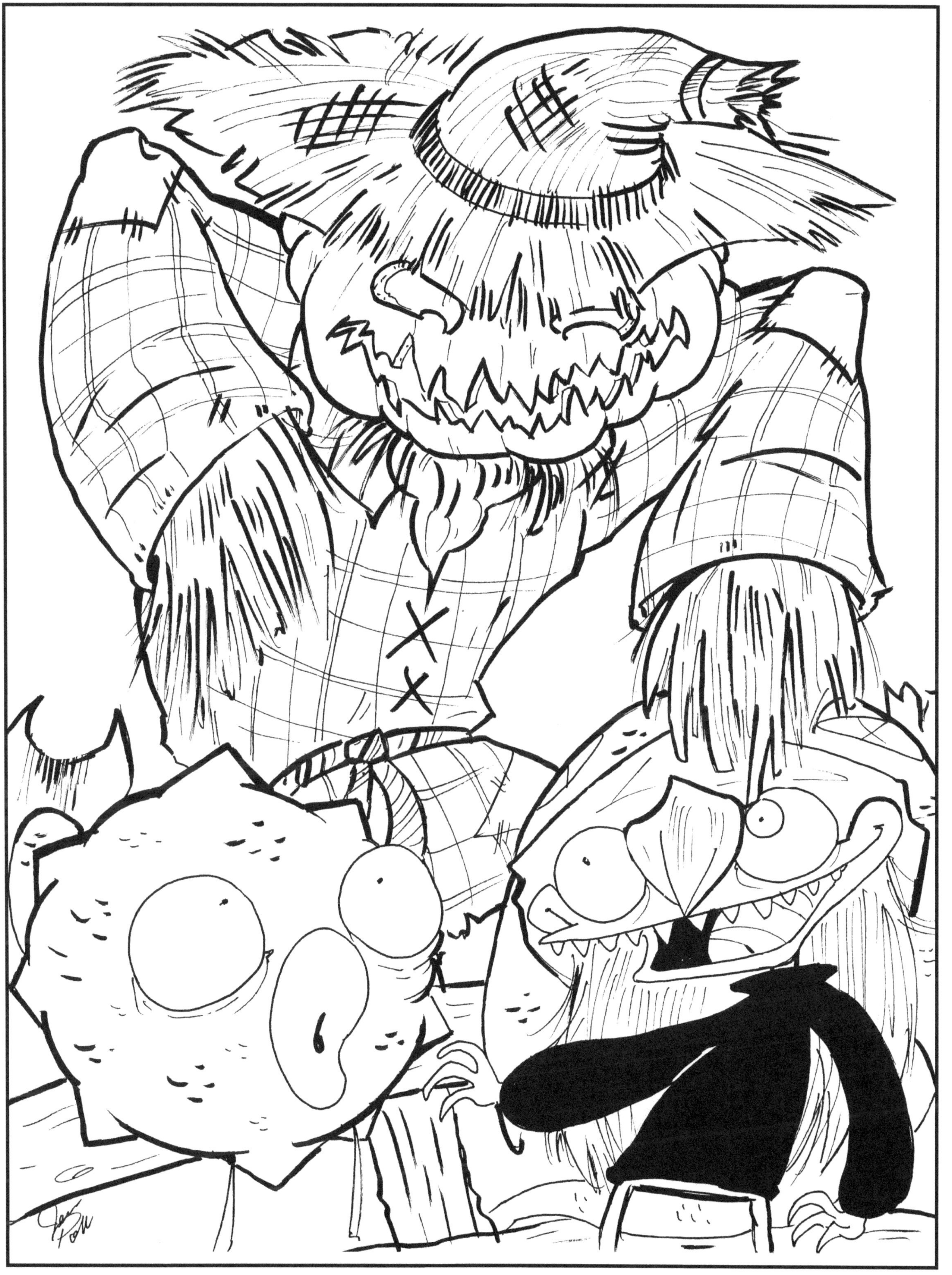

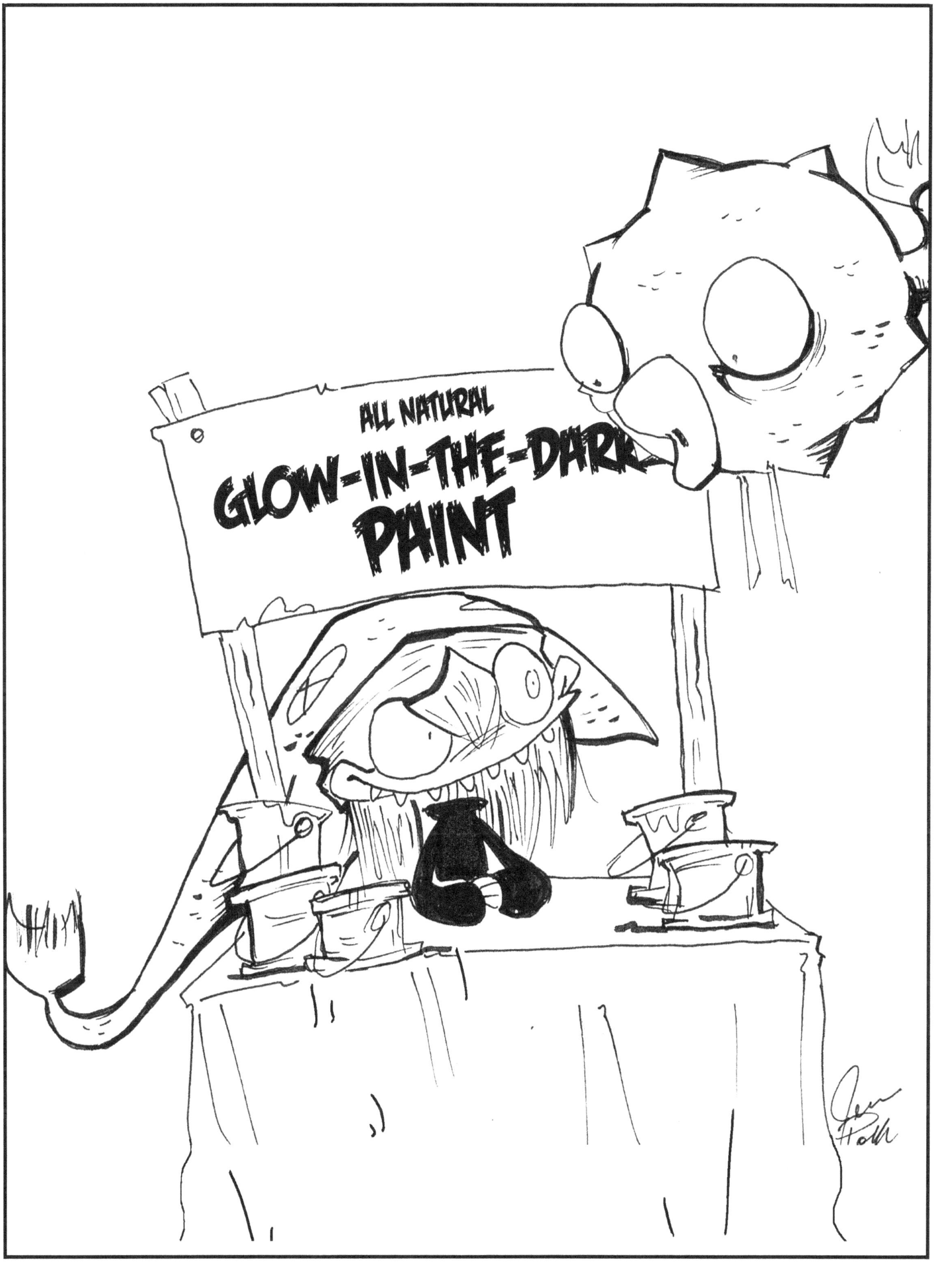
ALL NATURAL
GLOW-IN-THE-DARK
PAINT

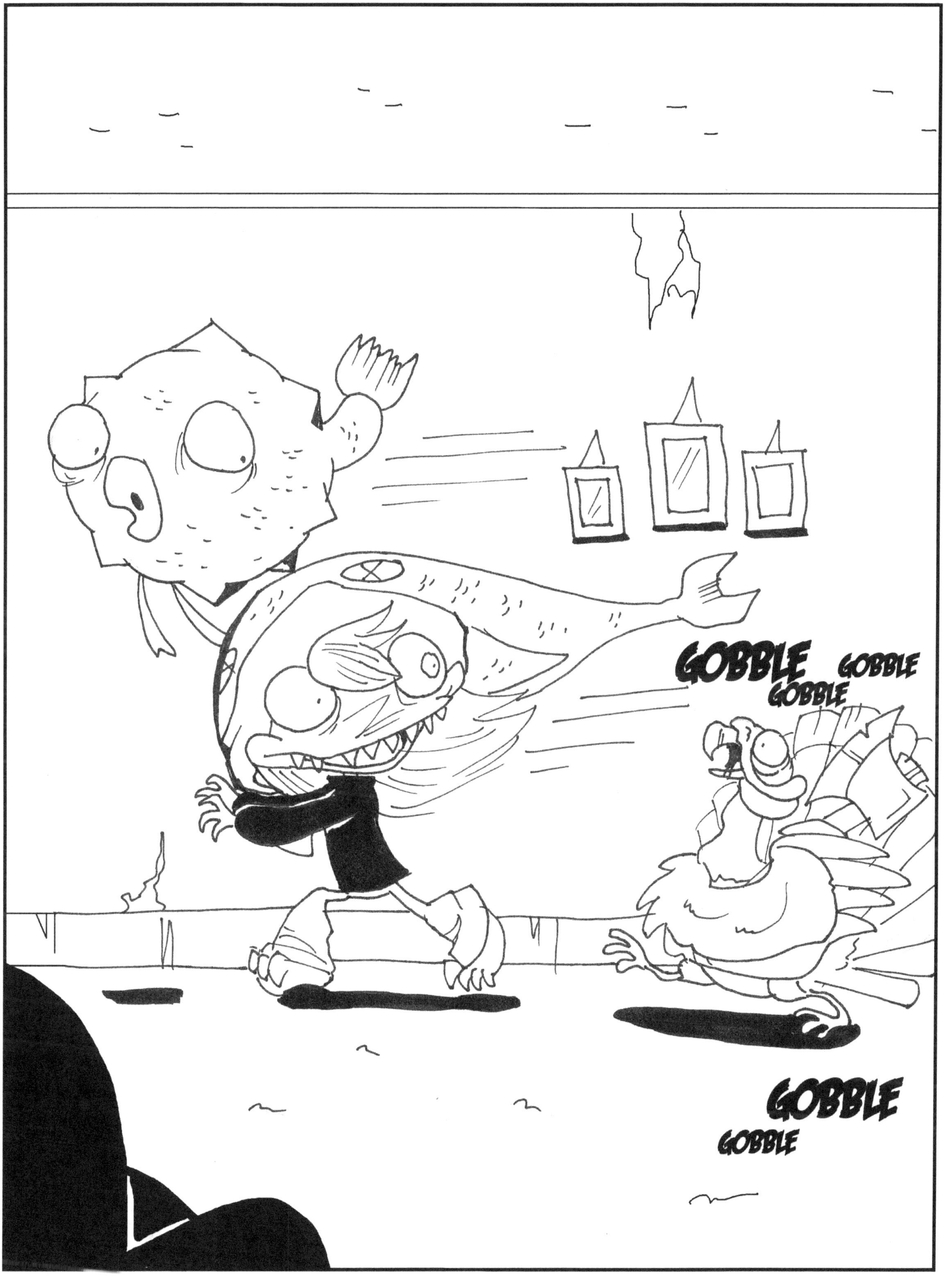
GOBBLE
GOBBLE
GOBBLE
GOBBLE
GOBBLE

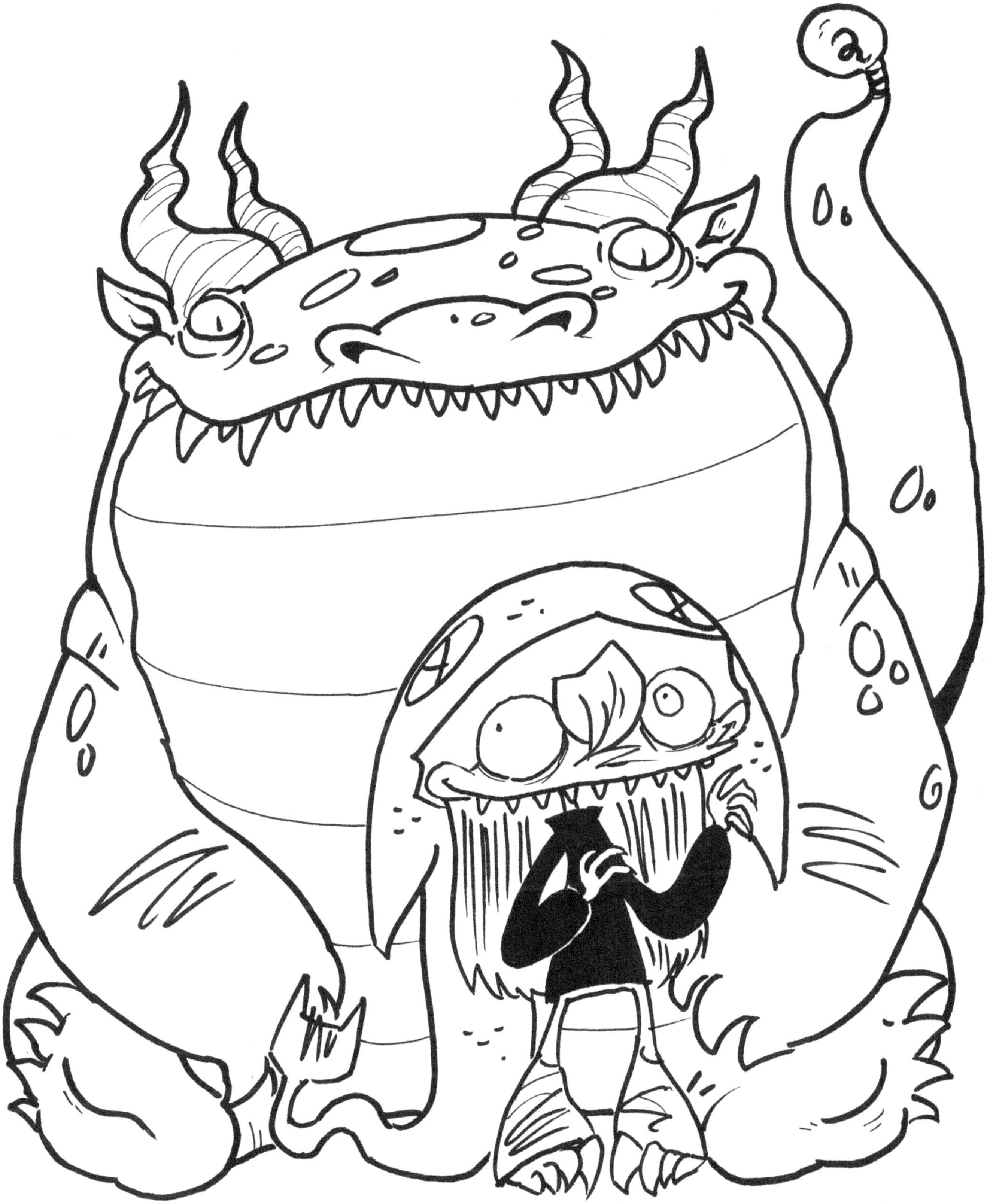

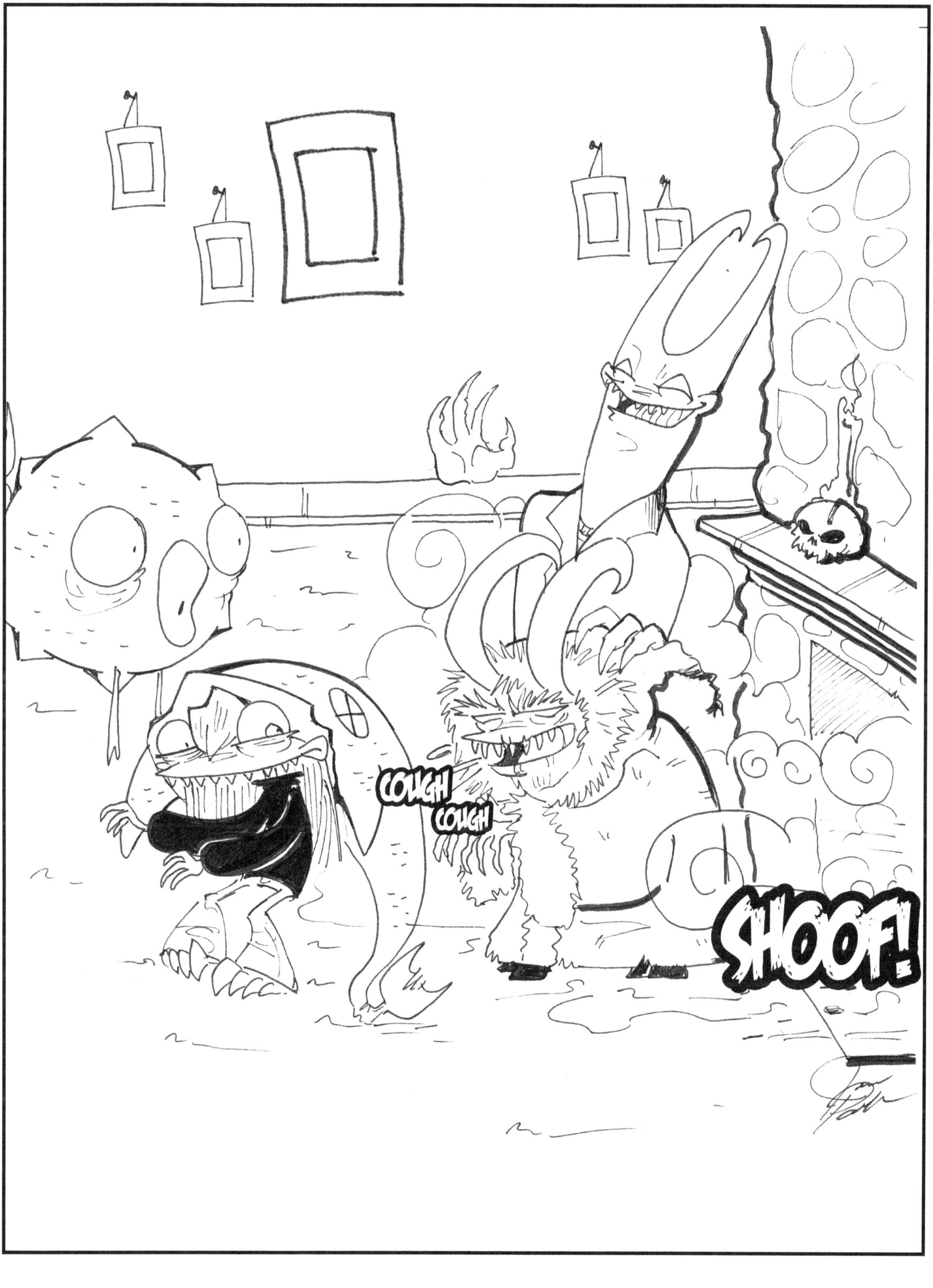
COUGH
COUGH
SHOOF!

www.ingramcontent.com/pod-product-compliance
Lightning Source LLC
Chambersburg PA
CBHW080531220526
45465CB00006B/2666
9798366818018